Protagoras

ANCIENTS IN ACTION

Boudicca
Marguerite Johnson

Catiline
Barbara Levick

Catullus
Amanda Hurley

Cleopatra
Susan Walker and Sally-Ann Ashton

Hadrian
James Morwood

Hannibal
Robert Garland

Horace
Philip D. Hills

Lucretius
John Godwin

Martial
Peter Howell

Ovid: Love Songs
Genevieve Lively

Ovid: Myth and Metamorphosis
Sarah Annes Brown

Pindar
Anne Pippin Burnett

Sappho
Marguerite Johnson

Spartacus
Theresa Urbainszyk

Tacitus
Rhiannon Ash

Protagoras

Daniel Silvermintz

Bloomsbury Academic
An imprint of Bloomsbury Publishing Plc

B L O O M S B U R Y
LONDON • NEW DELHI • NEW YORK • SYDNEY

Bloomsbury Academic

An imprint of Bloomsbury Publishing Plc

50 Bedford Square	1385 Broadway
London	New York
WC1B 3DP	NY 10018
UK	USA

www.bloomsbury.com

**BLOOMSBURY and the Diana logo are trademarks of
Bloomsbury Publishing Plc**

First published 2016

British Library Cataloguing-in-Publication Data
A catalogue record for this book is available from the British Library.

ISBN: PB: 978-1-47251-092-1
ePDF: 978-1-47251-111-9
ePub: 978-1-47251-262-8

Library of Congress Cataloging-in-Publication Data
A catalog record for this book is available from the Library of Congress.

Series: Ancients in Action

Typeset by Fakenham Prepress Solutions, Fakenham, Norfolk NR21 8NN
Printed and bound in India

Contents

Preface

> Most likely, though, Protagoras, being older, is wiser than we, and if, for example, he should emerge from the ground, here at our feet, if only as far as the neck, he would prove abundantly that I was making a fool of myself by my talk, in all probability, and you by agreeing with me; then he would sink down and be off at a run. (Socrates in Plato's *Theaetetus* 171c–d)

This book is a study of Protagoras of Abdera (c. 490–420 BC), the founder of the sophistic movement and one of the most controversial thinkers in the history of philosophy. Despite having acquired a cult-like following of devotees, many philosophers of the period dismissed Protagoras as a charlatan who was more concerned with obtaining riches than wisdom. This judgment of his character has surrounded Protagoras for much of the last two-and-a-half thousand years. To cite just one example, the following is a second-century AD assessment of the infamous thinker:

> This Protagoras was not a true philosopher, but the cleverest of sophists; for in consideration of the payment of a huge annual fee, he used to promise his pupils that he would teach them by what verbal dexterity the weaker cause could be made the stronger. (Gellius, *Attic Nights* 5.4.1)

In spite of the long-held prejudice against Protagoras, his relativistic first principles pose a serious challenge to the tradition of Western metaphysics. After suffering many years of vilification, Protagoras has recently been rediscovered by postmodern thinkers for having provided an alternative ground for philosophic speculation. In the wake of this resurgent interest in Protagoras, there is no better time to engage in a serious investigation of his life and thought.

Although many of Protagoras' ideas do not seem particularly

shocking to someone in the twenty-first century, they were absolutely groundbreaking in his own day. This begins with his agnosticism regarding the traditional Greek gods. Having concluded that it would be too difficult either to prove or disprove the existence of the gods, Protagoras summarily dismisses them as irrelevant and repositions human beings in their place as the sole arbiters of truth. In his most well-known aphorism, Protagoras declares, "Of all things the measure is Man, of the things that are, that they are, and of the things that are not, that they are not" (DK 80B1). This seemingly innocent attempt to dignify the human experience constitutes nothing less than a complete revaluation of all values. Rather than appealing to a transcendent realm of absolute truth, Protagoras affirms that there are as many truths as people in the world. This radical understanding of epistemology led him to an equally radical political theory. Protagoras is credited as the first thinker to provide a philosophic defense of democracy—the only regime that validates the thoughts and opinions of all of its citizens. Recognizing the value of persuasion within this contentious political climate, he taught the art of rhetoric and advocated its use as the best means for advancing one's interest over competing parties. Although an early proponent of public education for the poor, Protagoras won fame and fortune providing Greece's wealthy elite with the forensic skills to ascend the political ranks as powerful statesmen.

Protagoras was a prolific author publishing no less than thirteen works concerning theology, politics, ethics, and rhetoric. Unfortunately, only the titles of these works survive, leaving us to piece together his contributions from a handful of anecdotes about his life and from a fairly short collection of quotations found in other authors. The most significant of these sources are Plato's *Protagoras* and *Theaetetus*. In the dialogue named for him, Protagoras appears as a character and presents his ideas regarding ethics and politics in a passage known as the "Great Speech" (Plato, *Protagoras* 320c–328d).

Many scholars believe that Plato has faithfully preserved Protagoras' central ideas in this passage. In light of this scholarly consensus, my analysis will largely be based on an interpretation of this section of Plato's dialogue.

Although Socrates directly interrogates Protagoras following the "Great Speech," he is afforded much greater freedom in several other Platonic dialogues to scrutinize the sophist's ideas without him being there to defend himself. During one of these investigations, Socrates reveals that Protagoras had, in addition to his public discourse promoting morality, a less ethical secret doctrine that he shared privately with selected students. If Socrates' provocative claim is true, then we risk completely misunderstanding Protagoras if we do not go beyond the surface of what he says. Consequently, the book will conclude with a more speculative analysis of the secret doctrine concealed within the "Great Speech."

Chapter 1, "From Humble Beginnings to Celebrated Teacher," provides an intellectual biography of Protagoras by drawing on the surviving anecdotes about his life. This includes a detailed discussion of his education under the philosopher Democritus. In particular, the ethical and epistemological implications of Democritus' physics are considered in order to show how the materialist approach of the pre-Socratic natural scientists laid the groundwork for Protagoras' radical views on these subjects. This overview is followed by a discussion of Protagoras' emergence as a professional educator with special focus on his introduction of the practice of charging for instruction.

Chapter 2, "Protagoras and Pericles," begins with a careful examination of Protagoras' political thought. Having first clarified his defense of democracy, the chapter proceeds by showing how these ideas influenced Athenian political reforms as a result of his relationship with the statesman Pericles. The chapter closes with an investigation of how Pericles' abuse of power exposes the potential injustice of Protagoras' seemingly noble defense of equal rights for all citizens.

The concluding chapter, "Protagoras' Secret Teaching," begins by placing Protagoras in the history of esoteric thinkers. After establishing his use of esotericism in the "Great Speech," the chapter proceeds with an exegesis of his public discourse promoting morality. It is then shown how various anomalies within this account expose a less ethical secret doctrine. Despite Protagoras' eloquent and reasoned defense of traditional morality, the secret doctrine affirms that the best means for maximizing one's self-interest is to rule the city as a powerful statesman who stands beyond the law.

In a comical scene in Plato's *Theaetetus* (171c–d), the deceased Protagoras wakes from the dead and pops his head above ground just far enough to chastise Socrates for what he believes is a mischaracterization of his ideas. It is impossible to offer a completely objective interpretation of Protagoras' thought, and this work is no exception. Hopefully, Protagoras does not take too much offense from the grave at the critical assessment of his ideas presented in this book. If nothing else, I offer the following as one interpretation of his thought with the understanding that there are always many sides to an argument.

Acknowledgments

Nothing helps clarify a difficult thinker's ideas as much as teaching them to others. For this, I thank my students at the University of Houston-Clear Lake, especially Tammy Childress, Christopher Rhodes, Rebecca Franco-Garcia, Joshua Richards, Daniel Stuart, Ashleigh Godfrey, and Dru Watkins. Additionally, I thank friends from Lynbrook, Amherst, Annapolis, Irvine, Dallas, and Houston with whom I have discussed philosophy over the last 30 years. Several scholars have read parts of the manuscript, and I am grateful to Donald Kagan, Sarah Costello, and Laurence Lampert. I also thank my university for granting me a faculty development leave in order to work on this project. For general encouragement, I thank my mother-in-law, Marj Hales, and my parents, Carole and Joseph Silvermintz. Finally, I owe my greatest debt of gratitude to my wife and esteemed colleague, Barbara Hales.

Daniel Silvermintz
Houston, Texas
December 2014

Note on Sources

Modern scholarship is cited throughout the text using the author, date, and page number. All ancient sources are cited with line numbers, allowing readers to locate the passage both in the original text, as well as in any modern translation. In most cases, translations of ancient texts are quoted from the bilingual edition of the Loeb Classical Library published by the Harvard University Press. Translations of the pre-Socratic fragments, identified using the Diels-Kranz (DK) number, are quoted from Freemen's collection, *Ancilla to the Pre-Socratic Philosophers* (Cambridge: Harvard University Press, 1983). A complete list of all other translations can be found in the bibliography at the end of the work.

Note on Sources

From Humble Beginnings to Celebrated Teacher

I know of one man, Protagoras, who amassed more money by his craft than Pheidias—so famous for the noble works he produced—or any ten other sculptors. ... For I believe he died about seventy years old, forty of which he spent in the practice of his art; and he retains undiminished to this day the high reputation he has enjoyed all that time.

Socrates in Plato's *Meno* 91d

Humble beginnings

Several provocative anecdotes about Protagoras' life have been passed down to us scattered throughout the surviving ancient sources. The lengthiest ancient biography of Protagoras is found in a chapter devoted to him in Diogenes Laertius' third-century AD work, *Lives and Opinions of Eminent Philosophers*. Other valuable biographical details are provided by Plato, Aristotle, Gellius, Athenaeus, and Plutarch. It should be noted that many of these authors lived considerably later than Protagoras, and thus, did not have first-hand knowledge of him. Moreover, it is difficult to obtain an objective account of Protagoras' ideas when we must rely on the testimony of authors who oppose his philosophic standpoint. In spite of the challenges posed by the surviving sources, I will attempt to reconstruct a coherent narrative of Protagoras' formative education and professional career as an educator, rhetorician, sophist, and political theorist.

Protagoras' parents must have had high aspirations for their son when giving him such an auspicious name. The name Protagoras is derived from two Greek words: *protos* (first) and *agoreuo* (to speak in public, especially in the assembly) (Liddell et al. 1940). As happenstance has it, his name encapsulates his many accomplishments. He is arguably the first philosopher to offer a systematic treatment of ethics and politics. These investigations resulted in a number of other groundbreaking claims, including being the first philosopher to express his skepticism about the existence of the gods (DK 80B4; Plato, *Theaetetus* 162d–e), and the first to advocate for democracy (Plato, *Protagoras* 320c–328d). He was the first to acknowledge that he practiced sophistry, as well as the first to request fees for his instruction of others in this art (Plato, *Protagoras* 317b). Finally, as one of the period's most famous teachers of rhetoric, Protagoras holds first place in the ranks of the orators.

Protagoras was born in Abdera, a Greek city on the southern coast of Thrace, around 490 BC.[1] Although Abdera was the home of several famous philosophers and scholars, the citizens of the city had a reputation for ignorance as indicated by the derogatory associations of the word Abderite (Smith et al. 1890: 2). Seeking refuge during the Persian Wars, many Greeks fled to Abdera, where they found security, as well as a thriving economy. One can also imagine that the colorful mix of people, cultures, and goods found in a place like Abdera provided fertile ground for a philosopher investigating human behavior.

Although Protagoras would later achieve great fame and fortune, he appears to have come from quite humble beginnings, working as a manual laborer. The philosopher Timon of Phlius (320–230 BC) describes Protagoras' rugged appearance: "a man with clear voice, eye straight on the mark, and able for any work" (Sprague 1972: 10). When considering Protagoras' economic status, one should keep in mind the value that the ancient Greeks placed upon civic engagement. A respectable citizen in the fifth century was expected to possess enough wealth so that he would be freed from the burdens of hard labor. Hanson (1999: 66–7) notes that most individuals in this period lived on a family farm where the majority of the work was carried out by slave labor. This economic arrangement allowed individuals to prioritize their participation in the public affairs of the city, whether this meant going off to war or helping deliberate policy on the homefront. Given the high social value that was placed upon civic engagement, the manual laborer was disparaged since his work prevented him from full participation in the political and social life of the city. Aristotle goes so far as to regard the artisan as holding a position lower than a slave:

> For the slave is a partner in his master's life, but the artisan is more remote, and only so much of virtue falls to his share as of slavery— for the mechanic artisan is under a sort of limited Slavery. (*Politics* 1260a–b)

As bad as things were for the artisan, Protagoras would have been held in even lower esteem as an unskilled laborer.[2]

Legend recounts that Protagoras began as a porter responsible for transporting heavy loads (Diogenes Laertius 9.8.53; 10.1.8; Gellius, *Attic Nights* 5.3; Athenaeus, *Deipnosophistae* 8.352d–358c).[3] One day while carrying out his duties, Protagoras was stopped by the philosopher Democritus (460–370 BC).[4] Although Democritus had disdain for most men on account of their frivolity (Aelian, *Historical Miscellany* IV.20), he was immediately impressed by Protagoras' intelligence in packing such a large bundle with a single piece of rope: "My dear young man, since you have a talent for doing things well," praised Democritus, "there are greater and better employ-ments which you can follow with me" (Gellius, *Attic Nights* 5.3.1).

Protagoras eagerly accepted the offer to escape his menial occupation and take up residence at the house of Democritus, where he was welcomed as a member of the family.[5]

Education under Democritus

We can assume that Protagoras received a broad and rigorous education under Democritus, who is regarded as one of the greatest minds of the period. Democritus was a prolific author, publishing important works on biology, mathematics, physics, astronomy, cosmology, geography, ethics, logic, grammar, poetry, and music, as well as an extensive list of technical manuals on various arts including farming, medicine, dietetics, painting, and military strategy (Diogenes Laertius 9.7.46–8). The wide-ranging catalogue of Democritus' writings is even more intriguing for the present investigation since Protagoras is reported to have worked for the philosopher as his secretary (Diogenes Laertius 10.8; Athenaeus, *Deipnosophistae* 8.352d). In light of this, one wonders to what extent Protagoras might have been responsible for authoring some of the works credited to his teacher. Whether or not this is the case, there are significant affinities between the two philosophers' ideas. It is thus valuable to have some understanding of Democritus' philosophy before engaging in a study of Protagoras' thought.

Although Democritus contributed to many fields of study, he is most known for his work on physics. The ancient Greeks not only created some of the most wonderful works of mythology, but also some of the earliest known scientific explanations of the natural world. Beginning in the sixth century BC, the first scientists proposed various material elements (water, air, fire, earth, or some combination of these) as constituting the totality of existing things. Aristotle summarizes the approach adopted by these thinkers:

Most of the earliest philosophers conceived only of material principles as underlying all things. That of which all things consist, from which they first come and into which on their destruction they are ultimately resolved, of which the essence persists although modified by its affections—this, they say, is an element and principle of existing things. (*Metaphysics* 983b)

Rather than appealing to a host of supernatural gods, the physicists sought to explain the world through empirical evidence and reason.

It is remarkable that the ethical, political, and religious implications of a world composed solely of unconscious elements do not appear to have come to light for several generations. This is likely explained by a certain affinity between the mythological understanding of nature and the approach adopted by the first scientists. In this regard, one should keep in mind that the Greek deities are not comparable with the invisible and intangible God of the Bible, but rather should be thought of as personified forces of nature. The Ancient Greeks need only look up to the sky to experience Zeus' wrath, manifest in every lightning storm. In light of this association between the divine and the natural world, it may not have seemed sacrilegious to appeal to material elements as responsible for the cosmic order. Some of the early scientists may even have considered the primal elements to have a divine status. This is, at least, the report of Diogenes Laertius regarding Thales, who is acknowledged as the first natural scientist: "His doctrine was that water is the universal primary substance, and that the world is animate and full of divinities" (1.1.27). It is understandable that Thales conceives of water as divine in light of its life-sustaining powers. Additionally, water appears imperishable as it continuously fluctuates through the three states of matter. Materialist physics and spirit-worship were, at least for Thales, not incompatible.[6]

Following the materialist approach adopted by Thales, subsequent thinkers sought to improve on his theory by offering additional

elements comprising the natural world. These rival theories culmi-
nated in the work of Democritus, who posited the existence of an
indivisible substance termed *atomos*—literally that which cannot
be further cut. Diogenes Laertius provides the following summary
of Democritus' physics: "His opinions are these. The first principles
of the universe are atoms and empty space; everything else is
merely thought to exist" (9.7.44).[7] In contrast to prior scientific
theories, Democritus does not grant divine status to the primary
elements.

Democritus' materialist physics presents a radically new
conception of the universe devoid of divine agency. Diogenes
Laertius explains what this entails: "All things happen by virtue of
necessity, the vortex being the cause of the creation of all things, and
this he calls necessity" (9.7.45). With no greater intentionality than
the motion of rebounding billiard balls, the reality that emerges out
of the colliding atoms is merely a product of the necessary cause and
effect by which some atoms adhere to one another while others are
repelled.

Democritus' understanding of physics led him to a radical
skepticism about our ability to obtain accurate knowledge of the
world. He affirms: "Man is severed from reality" (DK 68B6); "We
know nothing about anything really" (DK 68B7); "It will be obvious
that it is impossible to understand how in reality each thing is" (DK
68B8). Although we want to believe that our various perceptions
correspond with the external world, Democritus contends that
perception is merely an epiphenomenon of the influx of atoms. He

thus declares, "Sweet exists by convention, bitter by convention, color
by convention; atoms and Void (alone) exist in reality" (DK68B9).
Despite drawing different conclusions, Democritus' epistemological
scepticism is where we see his greatest influence on Protagoras.
While Democritus views the incapacity to obtain knowledge of the
world as a human deficiency, Protagoras celebrates humans as the

measure of all reality and dismisses any truth claims beyond this vantagepoint (DK 80B1).[8]

Ironically, the bulk of the surviving fragments of Democritus come from his ethical writings rather than from his works on natural science. In several hundred fragments, he promotes traditional moral maxims by exhorting individuals to moderate their desire for pleasure and riches. Democritus implores his readers: "Do not say or do what is base, even when you are alone. Learn to feel shame in your own eyes much more than before others" (DK 68B244). Assuming the authenticity of Democritus' ethical writings, it is difficult to reconcile these ideas with his physics. If the gods are not observing men's actions, then why indeed should one conduct oneself in an upright manner, especially when one stands to benefit from unjust behavior? As we shall see, Protagoras' covert defense of immorality is premised upon this fundamental ethical dilemma.

The unethical implications of Democritus' physics did not escape the playwright Aristophanes, who provides a scathing critique of the scientific enlightenment in his satirical play, *Clouds*, first performed in 423 BC. Exposing the impiety of the natural scientists, the character Socrates irreverently proclaims that Vortex has overthrown Zeus' reign; to which, his bumbling student Strepsiades retorts, "Vortex? I hadn't noticed that Zeus doesn't exist, and that instead of him Vortex is now king" (Aristophanes, *Clouds* 380).[9] With a fair bit of irony, Socrates now tries to initiate him in the new religion that follows from the scientific world view: "Now won't you believe in no god but ours: this Chaos, and the Clouds, and the Tongue, these three" (*Clouds* 423).[10] Regardless of whether Thales was serious when referring to all matter as divine, Aristophanes reveals the underlying contradiction of trying to wed the physics of natural science with any sort of ethical framework. He thus shows how Democritus' naturalistic understanding of the cosmos lays the foundation for

Protagorean relativism—the tongue being a clear allusion to the sophists' truth-twisting art of rhetoric. Democritus may exhort his readers to conduct themselves in an upright manner; nonetheless his physics have fundamentally undermined the transcendent basis of the ethical sphere.[11] Even though it may not have been his intention, Democritus provides the philosophic grounding for Protagoras' defense of immorality.

Celebrated teacher of rhetoric

After studying at the house of Democritus, Protagoras started his career as an educator in his own right. Athenaeus (*Deipnosophistae* 8.352d) reports that he initially taught reading and writing to people in remote villages.[12] This intriguing and underemphasized anecdote about Protagoras' commitment to educating the lower classes reveals a different side of his character than that which is typically thought about him. In fact, despite making his fortune from instructing the rich and famous, he never seemed to forget his own humble beginnings. With a sense of how Democritus' tutelage changed his own life, Protagoras was committed to providing this same opportunity to other less fortunate individuals.

Protagoras' education of the poor might be regarded as the first step in constituting a new form of government predicated on equal political rights for all individuals. Cuberley notes how traditional education functioned to maintain the power relations between the rich and the poor: "Education in Greece was essentially the education of the children of the ruling class to perpetuate the rule of that class" (1920: 20).[13] Protagoras challenged this hierarchical system, not only through his own tutelage of the poor, but also by developing governmental policy subsidizing public education for the colony of Thurii.[14]

Notwithstanding Protagoras' personal and political commitment to the less privileged, his success derived from tutoring Greece's wealthy elite. For this stratum of society, the newly developed arts of rhetoric and disputation were regarded as invaluable skills in helping one ascend the political ranks. Protagoras' expertise in these areas quickly made him highly sought after. Like many of the other sophists of the fifth century, Protagoras made his living traveling from city to city throughout Greece and its colonies. The sophist Hippias (460–400 BC), reports that Protagoras had, in particular, garnered a great reputation in Sicily (Plato, *Hippias Major* 282e). In addition, he spent considerable time in Athens, where his students included the playwright Euripides (480–406 BC), the rhetorician Isocrates (436–338 BC), and, most notably, the general and statesman Pericles (495–429 BC).

Several surviving fragments preserve Protagoras' philosophy of education: "Teaching needs endowment and practice. Learning must begin in youth" (DK 80B3); "Art without practice, and practice without art, are nothing" (DK 80B10); "Education does not take root in the soul unless one goes deep" (DK 80B11); "Toil and work and instruction and education and wisdom are the garland of fame which is woven from the flowers of an eloquent tongue and set on the head of those who love it" (DK 80B12). In describing the content of his instruction, Protagoras distinguishes his approach from that adopted by competing sophistic teachers. Protagoras charges that other sophists burden their students with more theoretical studies such as arithmetic, geometry, astronomy, and music. Rather than wasting his students' time with abstruse ideas, Protagoras promises his students that they will develop practical skills with tangible benefits:

Whereas, if he applies to me, he will learn precisely and solely that for which he has come. That learning consists of good judgement in his own affairs, showing how best to order his own home; and in the affairs of his city, showing how he may have most influence on public affairs both in speech and in action. (Plato, *Protagoras* 318e–319a)

Protagoras is not only the first philosopher to investigate human nature, but also appears to have developed a strategy for succeeding in life. Presumably, it was his promise to teach others his success strategy that attracted such a passionate group of disciples.

Although Protagoras affirms that education requires hard work, it is difficult to reconcile this sentiment with his promise to his students that they will make immediate gains following each day's instruction (Plato, *Protagoras* 318a–b). It is this latter claim that gives rise to the common criticism that the sophists teach a series of rhetorical tricks that could be learned by anyone rather than a serious academic subject requiring devoted study. In Plato's *Euthydemus*, Socrates debates two brothers who appear to have become accomplished sophists overnight. Although we do not know who instructed them, there are good grounds to speculate that it was Protagoras.[15] Having previously been competitors in a violent form of martial arts, these brutish fellows now fashion themselves as intellectuals who take down opponents with their rhetorical maneuvers and verbal dexterity: "wielding words as their weapons and confuting any argument as readily if it be true as if it be false" (Plato, *Euthydemus* 272a–b).[16] Not only have they achieved this level of expertise with apparent ease, Socrates reports that they promise to make others into sophistic fighters just as quickly as they acquired these skills: "they say it would take them but a little while to make anyone else clever in just the same way" (Plato, *Euthydemus* 272b).

The absurdity of sophists like Euthydemus and Dionysodorus claiming to make their students wise overnight raises one of the central critiques lodged against Protagoras, who was the first to have turned moral instruction into a commodity for sale (Plato, *Protagoras* 349a; *Hippias Major* 282c).This dubious practice earned him the nickname: "speech for hire" (*Suda* pi, 2958). Despite being a vigorous proponent of public education for the masses, Protagoras was not afraid to charge exorbitant tuition fees. Diogenes Laertius (9.8.52) reports that Protagoras had a set fee of one hundred minae. This is, to say the least, an extraordinary amount of money. To get a sense of just how prohibitive Protagoras' fees were, the average manual laborer is reported to have earned a daily wage equal to one hundredth of a mina (Glotz 1967: 174).

Protagoras' practice of requiring payment for instruction was quickly adopted by others and became a hallmark of the sophistic movement. This seemingly innocuous detail about this group of thinkers turns out to be one of its most controversial practices. Aristotle, in a well-known characterization of the movement, draws attention to the profit motive of these supposed intellectuals: "The sophist is one who makes money from an apparent but unreal wisdom" (*On Sophistical Refutations* 165a). Although the teaching profession endures scrutiny to this very day, most people would acknowledge that it is a noble vocation whose practitioners should be compensated for their labors. In contrast, the sophists were regarded by their contemporaries as fraudulent merchants, who either commodified something that should be bestowed freely or, even worse, taught others how to use various techniques of deception for the sake of unjust gain. Socrates, who was mistaken by the Athenian people to be a sophist, was accused during his trial to have charged for his instruction; in reality, he was an outspoken and harsh critic of this practice. He goes so far as to compare the sophist's sale of wisdom to the prostitute's commodification of affection:

> It is common opinion among us in regard to beauty and wisdom that there is an honorable and a shameful way of bestowing them. ... So is it with wisdom. Those who offer it to all comers for money are known as sophists, prostitutors of wisdom, but we think that he who makes

a friend of one whom he knows to be gifted by nature, and teaches
him all the good he can, fulfils the duty of a citizen and a gentleman.
(Xenophon, *Memorabilia* 1.6.13)

Traditional societies passed down their belief system from one
generation to the next through their political, cultural, and religious
institutions. As Socrates indicates, it was the role of every respectable
citizen to participate in the civic life of the community and to help
educate the next generation.[17]

The sophists responded to the criticism lodged against them
by arguing that they possessed technical knowledge akin to other
kinds of expertise. Just as someone would learn a trade by studying
under a practicing professional, the sophists contended that virtue
could similarly be acquired through formal instruction. Moreover,
if the craftsman should be compensated for selling his wares, so too
should a merchant of intellectual property be duly compensated
if one wishes to acquire his goods. In the course of admonishing
Socrates, Antiphon (480–411 BC) articulates the sophists' rationale
for charging their students:

> Socrates, I for my part believe you to be a just, but by no means a wise
> man. And I think you realise it yourself. Anyhow, you decline to take
> money for your society. Yet if you believed your cloak or house or
> anything you possess to be worth money, you would not part with it
> for nothing or even for less than its value. Clearly, then, if you set any
> value on your society, you would insist on getting the proper price for
> that too. (Xenophon, *Memorabilia* 1.6.11)

Antiphon contends that the value of ideas can be determined—just
like other commodities—by the price that consumers are willing to
pay for them.

If read literally, Protagoras' human-measure fragment seems to
encapsulate the sophistic conception of the role of the market in
assessing values: "The human being is the measure of all *chremata*

(valuable things)" (DK 80B1).[18] Rejecting the notion of universal truth, Protagoras is affirming that each individual must judge the truth of things for himself. Although translators of the fragment typically render *chremata* as "things," the word more literally means valuables or money.[19] If the human-measure fragment is translated in this manner, then Protagoras is suggesting that one way in which individuals measure the world is by assigning monetary values to goods.

Protagoras thus interpreted the public's willingness to pay his high tuition fees as validation of his wisdom. Socrates reports that Protagoras became one of the wealthiest individuals in the ancient world as a result of his 40 years teaching sophistry and rhetoric (Plato, *Meno* 91d). Moreover, he appears to have been a fairly shrewd businessman. One example of this was his offer of a money-back guarantee to any unsatisfied customer. Protagoras explains his financial agreement with his students: "When anyone has had lessons from me, if he likes he pays the sum that I ask; if not, he goes to a temple, states on oath the value he sets on what he has learnt, and disburses that amount" (Plato, *Protagoras* 328b–c).[20] In contrast to other academic studies, Protagoras argues that the sophistic art has practical application and wants his students to realize its benefits. He had therefore brokered an agreement with his student Euathlus that he pay part of his tuition up front and render the remainder only after he had applied his newly acquired knowledge to win his first lawsuit. Despite agreeing to these terms, Euathlus cleverly tried to avoid paying the outstanding fees by forestalling his career in the law courts. Protagoras understandably wanted the money owed him and resorted to suing Euathlus in what would become a well-known legal case.[21]

In probably the most amusing of the surviving anecdotes, Protagoras failed in his attempt to recoup his money as Euathlus outsmarted the master rhetorician at his own game. We are fortunate to possess the speeches delivered by both litigants before the court. In these masterful examples of the eristic method, the two speakers have employed sophistic logic so that even a losing position can result in victory. Protagoras directly addresses the defendant with what he believed would be a foolproof argument:

> Let me tell you, most foolish of youths, that in either event you will have to pay what I am demanding, whether judgment be pronounced for or against you. For if the case goes against you, the money will be due me in accordance with the verdict, because I have won; but if the decision be in your favour, the money will be due me according to our contract, since you will have won a case. (Gellius, *Attic Nights* 5.10.1.407)[22]

Protagoras' argument presents the jury with a paradox: if he wins the case, then Euathlus must pay the outstanding fees in accordance with the court's judgment; if he loses, then Euathlus must pay based on the conditions of their original contract. Had Protagoras not been such a good instructor of rhetoric, he might indeed have won the suit; unfortunately, the well-trained Euathlus turned the tables on his teacher using the very logic that he learned from him. Euathlus offered the court the following counter argument in his defense:

> So let me tell you in turn, wisest of masters, that in either event I shall not have to pay what you demand, whether judgment be pronounced for or against me. For if the jurors decide in my favor, according to their verdict nothing will be due you, because I have won; but if they give judgment against me, by the terms of our contract I shall owe you nothing, because I have not won a case.

Responding to Protagoras with even more specious logic, Euathlus argues that if he were to lose the case, the conditions of the original contract would not be satisfied; however, if he were to receive a favorable judgment by the court, then the original contract should be regarded as null and void. The jury was so confused by the paradoxes raised by both litigants that they failed to issue any judgment in the case, and thus Euathlus won by default. Gellius concludes the anecdote arguing that Protagoras got what he deserved for having taught such specious logic in the first place: "Thus a celebrated master of oratory was refuted by his youthful pupil with his own argument, and his cleverly devised sophism failed" (*Attic Nights* 5.10.1).

Protagoras' disciples

Despite Protagoras' exorbitant fees, he appears to have developed a near cult-like following. Ambitious young men were desperate to obtain the sophistical and rhetorical skills that would facilitate their ascendancy in the political assembly. Plato's *Protagoras* captures the frenzy that surrounded the sophist during one of his trips to Athens.[23] In the opening scene of the dialogue, the reader encounters Socrates being awakened in the middle of the night by his friend Hippocrates. Appearing to have directed his teenage hormones to obtaining, of all things, knowledge of sophistic rhetoric, Hippocrates tells Socrates that he was possessed with an uncontrollable desire to meet with Protagoras upon learning of his sojourn in Athens. In fact, he reports that his urge was so strong that he had considered foregoing sleep despite having just returned from a long journey in a state of exhaustion. Although he resists this temptation long enough to get a few hours of shuteye, he awakens with a renewed mission that he must immediately become one of Protagoras' disciples. Frantically banging on Socrates' door with his walking stick, Hippocrates cries out in a loud voice: "Are you awake, or sleeping?" (Plato, *Protagoras* 310b). Obviously, Socrates was no longer asleep amidst all this commotion and welcomed his distressed friend in spite of the inappropriate hour. When Hippocrates reveals that his crisis is his urgent need to meet with Protagoras, Socrates assumes that the sophist must have wronged him. With a maniacal chuckle and a

solemn oath to the gods, Hippocrates affirms—like a spurned lover—
that he has indeed been wronged: "Yes, by the gods!" and, moreover,
that Protagoras is the one at fault for hoarding his knowledge: "by
being the only wise man, and not making me one" (Plato, *Protagoras*
310d). Although Socrates assures the young man that he need only
pay Protagoras his tuition fee to obtain his wisdom, he also cautions
him to be careful that he does not damage his soul when exposing
himself to the sophist's immoral ideas.

Hippocrates' response to Socrates reveals the ambiguous and
conflicted reputation of the sophists. On the one hand, he is
ashamed to become a sophist himself through associating with
Protagoras; on the other hand, he is unabashed about his desire
to become a persuasive speaker (Plato, *Protagoras* 312b–d). Even
if the sophists had somewhat of a questionable reputation, there
is certainly nothing shameful about being a great orator. On the
contrary, this is the sort of skill that any respectable citizen hoping
to make a name for himself in the assembly would be expected to
possess.[24] When Hippocrates later meets Protagoras, the sophist
reassures him that he should not be ashamed to learn the sophistic
art since it will, contrary to popular belief, make him a more
virtuous person:

> Young man, you will gain this by coming to my classes, that on the day
> when you join them you will go home a better man, and on the day
> after it will be the same; every day you will constantly improve more
> and more. (Plato, *Protagoras* 318a–b)

Although Protagoras is pretty vague about how his instruction will
improve Hippocrates, he does make a good sales pitch. He assures
Hippocrates that his students make tangible gains with each day's
instruction. Moreover, he backs up this promise with his money-back
guarantee in which the student only pays what he believes to be the
value of the instruction received.

With such grand promises, one can understand how Protagoras drew such a large and enthusiastic following. Moreover, Protagoras' claim to engender virtue in his students appears to have brought some level of respectability to the profession of sophistry. Young men eagerly sought out his instruction and, in turn, parents paid his high tuition fees with the hopes that their children would rise to prominence by mastering the rhetorical and forensic arts. One of Protagoras' most famous patrons in Athens was Callias III.[25] In fact, the two were so close that Protagoras appointed Callias guardian of his children upon his passing (Plato, *Theaetetus* 165a).Callias' obsession with the sophists was notorious in the ancient world. He appears to have set up his home as a sophistic academy, replete with lecture rooms and a dormitory to house the itinerant teachers during their sojourns in Athens. Moreover, he is reported to have spent more on the sophists than all of their other devotees combined (Plato, *Apology* 20a; *Cratylus* 391c; Xenophon, *Symposium* 1.5, 4.62). These expenditures were so significant that he went from being one of the wealthiest men in Athens to ending his life in abject poverty (Lysias, 19.48; Andocides, *Speeches* 1.131).[26]

Not surprisingly, Socrates and Hippocrates found Protagoras at the house of Callias. As it turns out, they also happened upon a number of other notable figures of the sophistic movement including Hippias and Prodicus (465–415 BC). Mistaking Socrates and Hippocrates as sophists soliciting work, Callias' doorkeeper initially turns them away since the house was already full to capacity (Plato, *Protagoras* 314d). When Socrates and his companion are finally granted entry, they witnessed each of the famed sophists lecturing before a group of devoted students. Socrates captures the intense scene surrounding Protagoras:

> and when we had entered, we came upon Protagoras as he was walking round in the cloister, and close behind him two companies were

walking round also; on the one side Callias, son of Hipponicus and his
brother on the mother's side, Paralus, son of Pericles, and Charmides,
son of Glaucon, while the other troop consisted of Pericles' other
son Xanthippus, Philippides, son of Philomelus, and Antimoerus of
Mende, who is the most highly reputed of Protagoras' disciples and
is taking the course professionally with a view to becoming a sophist.
(Plato, *Protagoras* 314e–315a)

As is evident from Socrates' description, Protagoras' students and
devotees came from some of the most illustrious Athenian families,
including the children of the general and statesman Pericles.[27]
The students were so packed around Protagoras that those on
the outside of the circle could barely hear him; nonetheless, they
were, according to Socrates, absolutely mesmerized by his teaching:
"enchanting them with his voice like Orpheus ..." (Plato, *Protagoras*
315a). What in the world was Protagoras teaching these young men
that would have them so captivated? What sort of knowledge could
possibly have so much draw on a teenager that it would send him
into a drunken frenzy to possess it? Why were families willing to
hand over their life savings to pay Protagoras' tuition fees? Although
we can piece together some answers to these intriguing questions,
some of Protagoras' most provocative and subversive teachings may
forever remain a mystery since he appears to have disseminated
one set of ideas publicly and a different set of ideas in private to his
paying students.[28]

Protagoras' secret doctrine

Despite the challenge, any attempt to reconstruct Protagoras' ideas
must go beyond his public discourse to speculate about his secret
doctrines. In Chapter 3, I provide a detailed analysis of both his
public discourse, as well as a more speculative account of his secret

doctrines. For now, I provide the following brief sketch of both his public and private teaching in anticipation of my more detailed discussion.

Protagoras' public teaching is best represented by what has come to be known as the "Great Speech" in Plato's eponymously named dialogue (*Protagoras* 320c–328d). Attempting to prove that morality is indeed a teachable subject, Protagoras delivers a masterful argument by drawing on both faith and reason to make his point. He begins his discourse with a mythic fable that strategically positions himself in the mind of the audience as promoting orthodox religious beliefs consistent with all ancient Greek city-states. Justice, according to Protagoras' myth, was bestowed as a gift of Zeus to all of humanity (*Protagoras* 322d). Having made this appeal to traditional religious belief, Protagoras turns to an empirical analysis of social practices to bolster his claim about the universality of virtue. Since all individuals within a community are expected to profess their uprightness, then it must be the case that all individuals have a capacity for such behavior (*Protagoras* 323a–e). Despite possessing this capacity for ethical action, Protagoras contends that virtue is not innate, but rather acquired through the socialization process. From the time children are young through their integration as fully functioning members of the community, they are acculturated in what the community deems praiseworthy and blameworthy. Furthermore, all of the society's cultural and social institutions function to reinforce these values through a system of reward and punishment. For Protagoras, the sophists' promise of teaching the young virtue is nothing other than what is expected of all citizens. Who could find fault with Protagoras when his professed aim in his public teaching is to aid the traditional religious and cultural institutions by promoting morality?

Although many readers of Plato's *Protagoras* are left with a positive impression of the sophist as a promoter of morality, closer analysis of the "Great Speech" reveals a much more subversive understanding of ethics and politics. This begins with his disingenuous attempt to align himself with traditional religious beliefs when he has explicitly stated that he is unsure of the existence of the gods (DK 80B4). Furthermore, the myth itself contains suspicious elements that undermine the claim that morality is sanctioned by the gods. Prior to Zeus and Hermes bestowing justice upon mankind, Prometheus steals knowledge of the technical arts from the other gods and provides humanity with this ill-gotten gain (*Protagoras* 321c–d). Not only does the myth establish that the gods exhibit injustice, but it also appears to grant immorality a more primordial role for humans than justice. Individuals consequently need to be taught justice despite not needing any similar education in injustice. This subtle reading of the "Great Speech" reveals the secret doctrine that justice and other notions of traditional morality are, in reality, merely social constructs. In this regard, Protagoras' human-measure fragment is accurate insofar as whatever a society determines to be just is true for as long as the society declares it to be so.[29] It also follows from Protagoras' maxim that the individual measuring the truth of things will inevitably be in conflict with his society since injustice is both more natural and more advantageous than justice. The student of Protagoras' secret doctrine not only learns why the pursuit of injustice is valid, but also how he can use sophistry and rhetoric to manipulate others so that he can commit injustice with impunity.

Protagoras and Pericles

*For I claim that whatever seems right and honorable to a state is
really right and honorable to it, so long as it believes it to be so; but
the wise man causes the good, instead of that which is evil to them
in each instance, to be and seem right and honorable.*

Protagoras as quoted by Socrates in Plato's *Theaetetus* 167c

The first democratic philosopher

Although democratic reforms arose in Greece as early as the
sixth century BC, Protagoras was the first philosopher to explain
the rationale of having a government ruled by its people. In an
often-cited passage, Cynthia Farrar goes so far as to acknowledge
Protagoras as "the first democratic political theorist in the history
of the world" (1988: 77). It goes without saying that this is no
small distinction. Although there is a widespread belief among
modern Western nations that democracy is the only valid form of
political rule, the idea of self-governance was a revolutionary idea
in the ancient world. For ancient societies, politics was inseparable
from religion. The gods were believed to have ordained what is
permitted and what is forbidden, as well as to have appointed rulers
responsible for upholding these precepts. To constitute a regime
in which mortal men, rather than gods, determined right and
wrong required nothing short of the dismantling of the traditional
understanding of man's place in the cosmic order and a totalizing
reconceptualization of a world without divine agency. Such a

radical re-envisioning of the world would require a thinker as bold as Protagoras to affirm that human beings are, in reality, the only measure of everything.

Historians of philosophy have tended to focus on Protagoras' contributions to epistemology and rhetoric despite the fact that political thought was one of his primary scholarly interests. In fact, this should probably be regarded (in light of Farrar's claim), as his most important contribution to the history of ideas. He published several now lost works on politics including *Controversies*, *Concerning the Political Order*, and a work on the pre-political state of man.[1] Moreover, many scholars believe that Plato has faithfully preserved Protagoras' political thought in the "Great Speech" (*Protagoras* 320c–328d). Drawing on both the "Great Speech," as well as other surviving fragments, we are able to piece together Protagoras' defense of democracy. More importantly, Protagoras' relationship with the fledgling Athenian democracy allows us to examine the real world application of these ideas.[2]

Athens was the intellectual epicenter of the Western world in the mid-fifth century, providing fertile ground for Protagoras and the other sophists to spread their controversial ideas. In fact, it was in Athens that Protagoras offered the first public reading of his sacrilegious treatise questioning the existence of the gods (Diogenes Laertius 9.8.53). Beyond the intellectual openness of Athens, Protagoras enjoyed special privileges within the city on account of his close association with Pericles—arguably the most powerful political figure of the fifth century. One of the most famous anecdotes about Protagoras records that he spent an entire day training Pericles in the art of sophistic rhetoric (Plutarch, *Pericles* 36.3). This intriguing story leads us to wonder to what extent Protagoras' political ideas influenced the statesman's revolutionary policies.

The chapter begins with an outline of Protagoras' political thought.

This is followed by a consideration of his influence on Pericles. Having applied the lessons of his sophistic education to the real political arena, Pericles allows us to assess the virtues and the vices of Protagoras' ideas. It was under Pericles' leadership that Athens had introduced democratic reforms; however, it was also under Pericles' leadership that Athens emerged as a power-hungry empire that sought to subjugate smaller Greek city-states.[3] The chapter concludes by considering how Pericles' abuse of power reveals the unjust implications of Protagoras' political thought.

Protagoras' political thought

Protagoras was not only the first, but also one of the few ancient philosophers to have defended democracy. Many philosophers of the period (Plato being the most notable example) were, in fact, staunch critics of the idea of self-governance. Protagoras' biography (as discussed in the previous chapter) sheds light on his uncharacteristic political orientation. Having come from a working-class background, he had a unique perspective for an intellectual of the period. Additionally, his hometown of Abdera was one of the earliest cities to adopt democratic reforms as is evident in their procedure for conducting legal trials.[4] Early in the fifth century, the city instituted a policy requiring a quorum of five hundred jurors to prosecute a death-penalty case. Although wealthy Athenians resisted democratic reforms, there appears to have been greater public support for reforms in Abdera. This was at least the sentiment of Democritus, Protagoras' teacher and fellow Abderite. Despite being of considerable means, Democritus here aligns himself with the poor majority: "Poverty under democracy is as much to be preferred to so-called prosperity under an autocracy as freedom to slavery" (DK 68B251).[5]

Protagoras' political thought follows from his philosophic first principle that the human being is the measure of truth (DK 80B1). Many individuals today would take for granted the idea that life is largely a product of human devising. This was, however, not how reality was perceived in the ancient world. In this period, religion functioned as a totalizing institution that regulated every aspect of life. In the political sphere, it was an unquestioned belief that the gods had determined right and wrong, and that it was an individual's role to uphold what had been divinely sanctioned. Protagoras' contention that human beings are the sole arbiters of truth amounted to a complete renunciation of the religious worldview and the ancestral tradition. Jacqueline de Romilly notes the revolutionary implications of Protagoras' repositioning of human beings in the production of knowledge:

> Man is what matters. What this means is that Protagoras jettisons all notions of being and truth that are in any way connected with the gods. In other words, at a single stroke he sets up a new universe in which the gods have no part to play. (1992: 102)

Protagoras confirms Romilly's suspicions in his famous declaration of agnosticism: "About the gods, I am not able to know whether they exist or do not exist" (DK 80B4). He additionally informs us that his omission of any reference to the divine in the human-measure fragment was not done unintentionally, but rather is consistent with one of his methodological precepts: "You bring in the gods, the question of whose existence or non-existence I exclude from oral and written discussion" (Plato, *Theaetetus* 162d-e).[6]

Although Protagoras is clear about the irrelevance of the gods for comprehending the world, it is not immediately obvious what he is proposing in their place. Interpreters throughout the ages have been frustrated by the inherent ambiguity of Protagoras' human-measure maxim: does he mean that each individual is a valid measure of truth, or that the collectivity of individuals constituting a distinct community define the truth for the individual? Moreover, if these are both valid interpretations of his maxim, then there is an obvious contradiction when the individual has views that contradict those upheld by his community. The apparent contradiction of the dual reading of Protagoras' maxim can be resolved if it is understood as an endorsement of democracy.[7] Although Protagoras asserts his maxim as a universal claim that applies to all forms of government, democracy is the only regime that resolves the tension between the individual and the collectivity by empowering the people to govern themselves. Protagoras explains the rationality of self-governance by arguing that all people possess the ability to deliberate political and ethical matters (Plato, *Protagoras* 322d–323c). He emphasizes democracy's reciprocal relationship in which the laws, which were formulated by the people, shape the succeeding generation of citizens: "the city sketches out for them the laws devised by good lawgivers of yore, and constrains them to govern and be governed according to these" (Plato, *Protagoras* 326d).[8]

Since all individuals have an equal capacity for virtue, it follows that all individuals should be equally entitled to share in the governing process. Although many might take this belief for granted today, this was quite a radical notion in the ancient world. Greek societies were stratified by a fairly rigid system that divided individuals into the wellborn nobility (*agathoi*) and the baseborn majority (*kakoi*). The rule of the nobility was legitimated with the belief that they alone possessed the mental ability to deliberate political affairs. The sixth-century lyric poet Theognis expresses the traditional views regarding the differing capacities of the *agathoi* and *kakoi* for sound judgment:

A good man (*agathos*), Kurnos, keeps his character in bad times and good; but if the God gives money and a good life to a bad man (*kako andri*), the fool cannot hold back his evilness. (Theognis 319–22)

Although the distinction between the *agathos* and the *kakos* was based on property ownership, Theognis indicates in a number of passages that the ignoble mental disposition is so ingrained in the *kakos* that he cannot change his social standing, even if his economic status were to change. Apparently, this mentality cannot even be influenced by the socialization process: "No one has ever found a way to make a fool wise or a bad man (*kakou*) good" (Theognis 430–2). In order to establish that all citizens are capable of sound judgment, Protagoras must prove false the traditional notion that virtue is an inheritable trait.

Protagoras proposes an ingenious thought experiment in order to establish that all individuals are capable of ethical action. Comparing the acquisition of morality to the process of learning a complicated skill, he has us imagine a society that devoted all of its educational efforts to train its citizens to be musicians:

> Suppose that there could be no state unless we were all flute-players, in such sort as each was able, and suppose that everyone were giving his neighbor both private and public lessons in the art, and rebuked him too, if he failed to do it well. (Plato, *Protagoras* 327a)

Despite all citizens in the musical city having similar opportunities, Protagoras contends that some individuals will prove to be better musicians than others on account of their natural inclination or their greater dedication to honing their skills. All the music lessons in the world will not make a tone-deaf individual into a virtuoso player. In spite of the fact that every citizen does not become a master musician, Protagoras argues that all citizens in the musical city will obtain a level of competency that will far exceed an individual raised in a nonmusical city:

Often the son of a good player would turn out a bad one, and often of a bad, a good. But, at any rate, all would be capable players as compared with ordinary persons who had no inkling of the art. (Plato, *Protagoras* 327a)

If we accept Protagoras' argument, then music should be considered a teachable skill since even the worst musician in the city has obtained a level of expertise as a result of being instructed.

Protagoras' argument suggests that people are mistaken about the inability to teach virtue because they are comparing it to a relatively simple skill in which we would expect that all learners will achieve absolute mastery. For example, we would not accept anything less than perfection from people when it comes to learning to walk. In contrast, we recognize that there will be a wide range of abilities displayed by those who have learned to play a musical instrument. Similarly, Protagoras argues that the range of ethical behaviors that result from the socialization process substantiates the conviction that ethics is teachable.

Protagoras' legitimation of the entire spectrum of ethical behaviors is nothing short of a revaluation of all values. He has effectively blurred the distinction between the nobility and the baseborn by acknowledging everyone who has undergone the socialization process as a valid ethical actor. Protagoras has us consider the relative virtue of the worst imaginable individual in a civilized society:

And you must regard any man who appears to you the most unjust person ever reared among human laws and society as a just man and a craftsman of justice, if he had to stand comparison with people who lack education and law courts and laws and any constant compulsion to the pursuit of virtue. (Plato, *Protagoras* 327c–d)

Protagoras' point is that even the worst individual is capable of receiving a moral education. He contends that every civilized society recognizes this notion as is evident in the significant efforts that are exerted to socialize individuals.

The final argument that Protagoras must address is how good policies are advanced in a democratic regime in the absence of an absolute standard of truth. Although one hopes that the deliberative process results in a majority opinion that is rational, history has shown that this is not necessarily the case. To return to Protagoras' analogy, we can expect that everyone in the musical city will be capable of playing his instrument, but there will only be a few great musicians. Likewise, everyone will have an opinion about political affairs in the democratic regime, but there will only be a few experts. We should no sooner expect that the majority of citizens in the democratic regime have reasoned opinions than expect beautiful music from the mediocre musicians in the musical city. Rather than denigrating the opinions of the masses, Protagoras maintains his position that each individual determines the truth for himself, though we often, as Socrates here observes, seek out the advice of experts:

> And we say that there is no one who does not think himself wiser than others in some respects and others wiser than himself in other respects; for instance, in times of greatest danger, when people are distressed in war or by diseases or at sea, they regard their commanders as gods and expect them to be their saviors, though they excel them in nothing except knowledge. (Plato, *Theaetetus* 170a)

Even the most self-assured individual (who otherwise believes himself to be the best judge of his affairs), will defer to an expert when facing imminent danger. Just as the sailors must respect the captain if they do not wish the ship to sink, so too must the passionate majority yield to the good counsel of the wise orator as he steers the ship of state through the rough waters of political turmoil (Plato, *Protagoras* 328b).

It should be noted that Protagoras is careful when introducing the role of the expert not to undermine his primary conviction that all individuals have an equal claim to the truth. Socrates here articulates Protagoras' position regarding the influence of the expert on the layman:

> And yet, in fact, no one ever made anyone think truly who previously thought falsely, since it is impossible to think that which is not or to think any other things than those which one feels; and these are always true. (Plato, *Theaetetus* 167a).

Everyone will admit it is better to be healthy than sick, but this does not negate the reality perceived by the sick person prior to following the advice of the physician. Likewise, Protagoras claims that the political expert can bring about a better state of affairs even if he does not possess a greater claim to truth than the rest of the city.

We may sum up Protagoras' political thought with the following points. No political regime has a greater claim to absolute truth; nonetheless, democracy emerges as the best regime since it is the only form of government that validates the thoughts and beliefs of the individual. Furthermore, since all individuals are capable of being taught ethical matters, everyone possesses the ability to participate in the political process. Although the individual remains the ultimate judge of what is true, it is the role of the wise orator to persuade the people so that their judgment corresponds with the best course of action for the good of the city.

Before commencing the "Great Speech," Protagoras promises that those individuals who study with him will obtain the skills to ascend the political ranks as powerful orators and statesmen. Protagoras claims that his student will learn, "how he may have most influence on public affairs both in speech and in action" (Plato, *Protagoras* 319a). Although Protagoras seems like he is making a general claim, several scholars contend that the passage alludes to his training of

Pericles, who is described by Thucydides (1.139.4) with the same phrase used by Protagoras (Segvic 2009: 17–20; O'Sullivan 1995: 20; Corrad 2013: 77).[9] Protagoras follows this with a more direct reference to Pericles, arguing in support of his theory that there is still hope that the statesman's children might someday be as great as their father (Plato, *Protagoras* 328c–d). Socrates then directly draws the connection between the sophist and the statesman, commenting at the conclusion of Protagoras' speech that it reminded him of one of Pericles' orations before the assembly (Plato, *Protagoras* 329a). In light of Plato's attempt to associate the sophist with the famous statesman, I now turn to an analysis of Protagoras' possible influence on Pericles.

Protagoras' education of Pericles

Although there is scholarly debate regarding the date of Protagoras' first visit to Athens, there is evidence suggesting this was as early as 460 BC.[10] The timing of this could not be more momentous in Athenian history. After some hundred years of ongoing political struggles, the democratic cause won a major victory with the dismantling of the Areopagus in 462 BC. Around this same time, Pericles inexplicably changed his political allegiance.[11] Despite being of considerable means and coming from one of Athens' most distinguished families, Pericles is reported by Plutarch to have suddenly sided with the poor masses rather than his fellow aristocrats: "then at last Pericles decided to devote himself to the people, espousing the cause of the poor and the many instead of the few and the rich, contrary to his own nature, which was anything but popular" (Plutarch, *Pericles* 7.2). Why did Pericles so abruptly change his political allegiance, especially when the democratic cause would seem to run contrary to his own interest? It does not appear that Pericles experienced a real change of heart. In fact, Pericles seems (at least in Plutarch's account), to have never actually believed in the popular cause that he is so famous for advancing. While we can only speculate, it is certainly possible that Protagoras had something to do with Pericles' shift in his political orientation.

Pericles' interest in ideas, and specifically, in philosophy is well documented. Not only did Pericles receive academic instruction as a young man, but he seems, less conventionally, to have continued his studies throughout his later years amidst the more practical business of leading military campaigns and helping to steer the ship of state (Plato, *Alcibiades 1* 118c). From all accounts, he was quite a serious student, having studied under the period's most prominent thinkers. He studied music with Pythocleides and also with Damon (500–415 BC), natural science, logic, and argumentation with Xeno (490–430 BC), physics with Anaxagoras (500–428 BC), and rhetoric and sophistic logic with Protagoras (Plutarch, *Pericles* 4.1–4; Smith 1844: 192). Plutarch notes how the study of philosophy shaped Pericles' character:

> Being gradually filled full of the so-called higher philosophy and elevated speculation, he not only had, as it seems, a spirit that was solemn and a discourse that was lofty and free from plebeian and reckless effrontery, but also a composure of countenance that never relaxed into laughter, a gentleness of carriage and cast of attire that suffered no emotion to disturb it while he was speaking, a modulation of voice that was far from boisterous, and many similar characteristics which struck all his hearers with wondering amazement. (Plutarch, *Pericles* 5.1)

Pericles represents an entirely new kind of ruler. His rise to power was not a result of his family lineage but rather resulted from his superior intellectual gifts.

Although Pericles studied a wide range of subjects, careful examination of his instructors indicates that all of his studies were premised on sophistic principles. Even if all the thinkers with whom Pericles studied are not typically classified as sophists, one should keep in mind that many thinkers who advanced sophistic ideas did not advertise this publically. Protagoras informs us that many sophists concealed their subversive ideas under the pretense of teaching socially accepted subjects such as music and poetry: "Now I tell you that sophistry is an ancient art, and those men of ancient times who practiced it, fearing the odium it involved, disguised it in a decent dress" (Plato, *Protagoras* 316d). Protagoras goes on to identify one of Pericles' music teachers, Pythocleides of Ceos, as one of these concealed sophists. Plutarch reveals his other music teacher, Damon, to have less successfully cloaked his subversive ideas behind music instruction: "However, Damon was not left unmolested in this use of his lyre as a screen, but was ostracized for being a great schemer and a friend of tyranny" (*Pericles* 4.2).[12] Isocrates also considers Damon to be a sophist and, much more surprisingly, adds the physicist Anaxagoras to the list of Pericles' sophistic instructors (*Antidosis* 15.235). Likewise, Timon of Phlius charges that Zeno's true gift was not in the area of natural science, but in sophistic rhetoric: "His was a tongue that could argue both ways with a fury resistless, Zeno's; assailer of all things" (Plutarch, *Pericles* 4.3).

With this broad outline of Pericles' sophistic influences, let us now turn to an examination of his relationship with Protagoras. One of the most famous anecdotes suggests that Protagoras was not only Pericles' teacher, but also a close associate. We are afforded a glimpse of this by Protagoras in an intimate account of his friend's state of mind at the passing of his sons, Paralus and Xanthippus, suggesting that the sophist was a part of the statesman's inner circle. The boys had both fallen victim to the second outbreak of the plague in 429 BC that ravished Athens and ultimately took Pericles' life. As it turns out, the passage is the largest surviving fragment attributed to Protagoras and thus merits extended quotation.[13] Protagoras describes the stately manner of his friend in the face of his tragic loss:

> His sons were comely youths, but though they died within seven days of each other, he bore their deaths without repining. For he continued to hold to that serenity from which day by day he added greatly to his credit of being blest by fortune and untroubled by sorrow, and to his high repute with the people at large. For each and every man, as he beheld Pericles bearing his sorrows so stoutly, felt that he was high-minded and manful and his own superior, being only too well aware of what would be his own helplessness under such circumstances. For Pericles, immediately after the tidings about his two sons, none the less placed the garland upon his head, according to the time-honored custom at Athens, and, clad in garb of white, harangued the people, taking lead in good counsel, and inspiriting the Athenians to war. (Plutarch, *Consolatio ad Apollonium* 33)

Along with the rest of Athens, Protagoras was clearly moved by Pericles' composure in the face of such a tragedy.[14]

Setting aside their personal relationship, I proceed to an analysis of how Protagoras' philosophical and political ideas influenced Pericles. To begin, we may assume (even in the absence of direct testimony), that Pericles was in attendance at Protagoras' reading of his work *On the Gods*. Diogenes Laertius provides three different reports as to where the reading took place, possibly suggesting that it received a public hearing on several occasions (Diogenes Laertius 9.8.54). Moreover, one of these reports places the infamous event at the academic, athletic, and military training facility known as the Lyceum. Pericles is reported to have maintained an office at this location, which allowed him both to oversee the training of the new class of warriors, as well as to attend lectures on science and philosophy.[15] Pericles' indebtedness to Protagoras' theological views is evident in a famous passage in which he declares his own beliefs about the gods: "The gods themselves we cannot see, but from the

honors which they receive, and the blessings which they bestow, we
conclude that they are immortal" (Plutarch, *Pericles* 8.6). Although
Pericles is more cautious than Protagoras not to appear impious, one
nonetheless hears echoes of the sophist's agnosticism in the statesman's inability to apprehend the gods directly.[16]

In addition to being exposed to his theological views, Protagoras
instructed the statesman in the art of rhetoric. This well-known
anecdote is helpful for both clarifying Protagoras' teaching method,
as well as the effects of this sort of training on such a powerful figure
as Pericles. Plutarch reports that the two men spent an entire day
discussing the following case of legal culpability:

> A certain athlete had hit Epitimus the Pharsalian with a javelin,
> accidentally, and killed him, and Pericles, Xanthippus said, squan-
> dered an entire day discussing with Protagoras whether it was the
> javelin, or rather the one who hurled it, or the judges of the contests,
> that 'in the strictest sense' ought to be held responsible for the disaster.
> (*Pericles* 36.3)

Protagoras' point in having Pericles think through this case is not, as
one might imagine, to have him ascertain which party is ultimately
responsible. On the contrary, Protagoras denies the existence of any
transcendent truth and, more specifically, denies that there is any
absolute reality to ethical, legal, or religious norms (Plato, *Theaetetus*
172b). For Protagoras, justice is nothing more than whatever a legis-
lative body, or jury, or religious institution declares it to be (Plato,
Theaetetus 167c, 172a, 177d).

Although Protagoras' critics might conclude that starting with
relativistic premises stifles one's ability to advance any position,
Protagoras adopts a quite pragmatic approach to this epistemological uncertainty. In the absence of absolute truth, one can still
discriminate between better and worse arguments. Of course, what
is more advantageous for one party will not be the same for another

party. In opposition to the entire philosophic tradition, Protagoras embraces the inherent contradictions that arise from conflicting interests and, consequently, the inevitable contentiousness of any argument. Diogenes Laertius summarizes Protagoras' rival philosophic approach: "Protagoras was the first to maintain that there are two sides to every question, opposed to each other, and he even argued in this fashion, being the first to do so" (9.8.51). Having renounced all claims to absolute truth, Protagoras trained his students to persuade others of their position, regardless of which side they were defending (Aristotle, *Rhetoric* 1452a; DK 80b6).

Returning to the case being discussed between Protagoras and Pericles, we can now see that this was a training exercise in argumentation that challenged the student to present equally persuasive arguments for all the implicated parties. With this sort of practical application in mind, Protagoras trained his students using legal hypotheticals such as the one discussed with Pericles.

Several other sophists had adopted Protagoras' method of training students. In a surviving manual composed by Antiphon of Rhamnus, we find a similar case to the one discussed by Protagoras in which a young boy was accidentally killed during javelin practice. Antiphon places the arguments of the respective litigants into the mouth of each boy's father. Although both fathers admit this was an unfortunate accident, they still argue that the opposing party's negligence was responsible for the death. After the father of the slain boy pleads for mercy, the other father turns the tables on him, arguing that not only is his son innocent, but that, in reality, he is the real victim here: "He did everything correctly, as he intended; and thus he was not the cause of any accident, but the victim of one, in that he was prevented from hitting the target" (Antiphon, *Speeches* 3.2.7). Although this seems like a completely absurd argument, many ancient accounts suggest that the sophists were so adept at arguing that they could successfully employ this sort of fallacious reasoning in real legal cases.

One can understand how being trained in this sort of forensic skill would benefit a statesman in his attempt to persuade the masses to adopt an unpopular policy. Plutarch comments that it was, in fact, Pericles' unrivaled rhetorical ability that won him the nickname Olympian Zeus. He further illustrates the point with an example that suggests Protagoras' influence. When Thucydides was asked whether he or Pericles was the better wrestler, he offered the following backhanded praise of his political rival: "Whenever I throw him in wrestling, he disputes the fall, and carries his point, and persuades the very men who saw him fall" (Plutarch, *Pericles* 8.4). Thucydides' description of his rivalry as a wrestling match seems to be referring directly to Protagoras, who often used physical sparring in his writings as a metaphor for various rhetorical manoeuvres.

One of the most famous anecdotes of the political rivalry between Pericles and Thucydides serves as a fine example of how Pericles applied his rhetorical skills to advance his policies. After Thucydides convinced the masses that Pericles was carelessly spending their money on his numerous public works projects, he won the people back with the following threat: "Let it not have been spent on your account, but mine, and I will make the inscriptions of dedication in my own name" (Plutarch, *Pericles* 14.2). This was all the people needed to reverse their sentiment and grant Pericles carte blanche to use the public funds as he saw fit.

Pericles and the struggle for democratic reform in Athens

Although Athens began instituting democratic reforms in the mid-sixth century under Solon (c. 638–558 BC), Pericles' innovative

policies in the mid-fifth century are credited with radically trans-
forming the political participation of the masses from a more
restricted and limited role to active engagement in the affairs of
the city. Despite being the originators and founders of the first
democratic regime, Athens was ridden with political strife as it oscil-
lated between democratic reforms and various forms of kingship,
aristocracy, oligarchy, and tyranny (Aristotle, *Athenian Constitution*
41).[17] In his political history of Athens, Aristotle records no less than
eleven constitutional changes from ancient times to his own day. It
will be useful to briefly trace the political history that set the stage for
Pericles to make the idea of democracy a reality.

Although Solon is recognized as the first democratic reformer, the
political regime he enacted was, in reality, more akin to an oligarchy
than a democracy. Prior to Solon's reforms, all power within Athens
was wielded by a few wealthy individuals, while the remainder of
society was relegated to a precarious position of serfdom. Without
land of their own, the poor were forced to rent land from the wealthy
to earn their daily bread. Since the debts of the poor were secured
with their personhood, the relationship of serf and overlord easily
degenerated into slavery when the renter was incapable of repaying
his debt (Aristotle, *Athenian Constitution* 2).

The desperate situation of Athens' poor finally came to a head
at the beginning of the sixth century as the people rose up against
their overlords. This uprising escalated into a full-blown civil
war between the rich and the poor. Both factions agreed to a
truce that would be mediated by Solon, who was committed to
representing both of the competing interests. Solon cancelled all
outstanding debts in an act known as the *Seisachtheia* (shaking off
the burdens). He additionally introduced a law that prohibited a
debtor from securing a loan with his personhood. Finally, Solon
drafted and introduced a new constitution replacing the laws of
Draco. Notwithstanding these significant advances, Solon could

only achieve so much. Despite granting the poorest citizens
the ability to participate in the political assembly and to serve
on juries, Solon's constitution reinforced the city's rigid stratification by restricting political offices to individuals based upon
an assessment of their annual income. Moreover, the opposing
parties that Solon tried to appease were never fully satisfied
with his concessions. Aristotle notes that the poor continued to
demand more radical property reforms while the wealthy resented
the financial losses they suffered with the absolution of all debts
(*Athenian Constitution* 11–13).

Even after adopting substantial reforms, Athens continued to
be plagued with civic strife and political turmoil. Once again, this
upheaval would only be resolved by the intervention of a strong
leader. In fact, even if Pisistratus (605–527 BC) was not despotic
in his rule, he is nonetheless a tyrant on account of the deceptive
means by which he seized power. Pisistratus was, like Solon before
him and Pericles after him, a complex and ambiguous character.
He was a populist who supported the interest of the poor, and
yet he undermined many of the key Solonian reforms that had
empowered the masses (Aristotle, *Athenian Constitution* 14–17).
Rather than granting the poor greater political participation, he
attempted to distract them from public affairs by bolstering their
personal finances. Despite curtailing public participation in this
way, Pisistratus was by all accounts a benevolent ruler. His sons, who
assumed rule over Athens following his death, did not possess either
the noble character of their father or his benevolent intentions. The
legacy following the reign of the house of Pisistratus served as an
important reminder to the Athenians throughout the fifth century
of the dangers of one man rule.

In the wake of the period of tyrannical rule, Athens was ready
for much more progressive reforms. Cleisthenes (570–508 BC)
significantly changed the political and social landscape through

a process of redistricting Attica in order to give greater representation to different factions within the city. These democratizing reforms were further concretized by Athens' transition from a land-based military to a naval power. In contrast to land battles that depended on a wealthy class of citizens with the resources to supply them with the hoplite armor, naval operations relied on brute man power. Enlisting its poorest citizens to man its war ships, Athens transformed the common man into a celebrated war hero.

In the period following the Persian Wars, Athens would experience both its rise to greatness as the cultural and intellectual epicenter of the Western world, as well as its subsequent fall at the hands of the Spartans in 404 BC. Pericles is responsible for much of Athens' preeminence. However he must also be held accountable for the overzealousness that resulted in its descent. In the wake of the Persian Wars, more than 150 autonomous Greek city-states united to form the military alliance known as the Delian League. Although the aim of the league was to thwart any future attempts by the Persians to subjugate Greek city-states, it effectively created an Athenian Empire that demanded tribute from smaller client states in the association. This role as a hegemonic power over the region was formalized as Pericles successfully relocated the alliance's command center and treasury from its home in Delos to Athens in 454 BC. Drawing on the resources of the Delian League, Pericles further expanded Athens' naval operations. No longer could the poor be dismissed as a burden on the community given their role in manning the war ships. Moreover, the ennobling of the masses through their involvement in naval operations bolstered their confidence to participate in all the city's affairs. After several generations of civic strife and class struggle, the time was ripe for more radical changes in the social and political landscape of Athens.

Even if the city was prepared for change, this could not have occurred without a charismatic leader capable of persuading the people to adopt these reforms. Under Pericles' leadership, Athens not only extended political rights to its poorest citizens, but also granted equal participation in the city's social and cultural life. The significance of Athenian democracy certainly did not escape Pericles, who famously celebrated its uniqueness in his funeral oration delivered at the end of the first year of the Peloponnesian War. In one of the most eloquent defenses of the superiority of democracy over other political constitutions, Pericles upholds Athens as a model for other Greek city-states to emulate:

> Our constitution does not copy the laws of neighboring states; we are rather a pattern to others than imitators ourselves. Its administration favors the many instead of the few; this is why it is called a democracy. If we look to the laws, they afford equal justice to all in their private differences; if to social standing, advancement in public life falls to reputation for capacity, class considerations not being allowed to interfere with merit; nor again does poverty bar the way, if a man is able to serve the state, he is not hindered by the obscurity of his condition. (Thucydides 2.36)[18]

Large-scale historical changes can never be explained by appealing to a single cause. As was evident in the outline of the historical events leading up to Pericles' rise to power, the poor had been clamoring for a more egalitarian society for several generations. They achieved significant social status with their participation in the naval battles in the Persian Wars and were further bolstered through Pericles' wide-scale expansion of the city's naval power. More importantly, Pericles was able to fund his various policies supporting greater public participation by drawing on the resources of the Delian League. Even with all of these pieces in place, democracy would never have emerged in Athens without a totalizing vision of how this new form of government would operate. We can only speculate to what extent the first philosopher of democracy might have influenced the first man of Athens in creating this new form of government.

The Protagorean roots of Athenian democracy

Protagoras' influence on Pericles' political thought is, perhaps, most evident in an exchange between the statesman and his ward Alcibiades. Attempting to catch Pericles in a contradiction about his political ideas, the ambitious Alcibiades confronts Pericles demanding to know what legitimates the legal order. With clear indebtedness to Protagoras, Pericles provides the following definition of a law: "You wish to know what a law is. Laws are all the rules approved and enacted by the majority in assembly, whereby they declare what ought and what ought not to be done" (Xenophon, *Memorabilia* 1.2.41). Surprisingly, Pericles makes no reference to either the gods or the ancestral tradition as providing a transcendent basis for legal precepts.[19] Pericles instead affirms Protagoras' radical conception that the consent of the community is the only arbiter of right and wrong. He concludes by defending the superiority of democracy over other regimes since the ruling majority only needs to impose its will on a small segment of the population.

Although Protagoras affirms that the community is the measure when constituting the legal order, he also recognizes that individuals will have different thoughts, feelings, and emotions. In all other regimes besides democracy, the majority of individuals must suppress their feelings and yield to the powerful minority. For the first time in history, Athenian democracy allowed the thoughts and feelings of the masses to be affirmed as valid. More than any of Athens' previous reformers, Pericles integrated the masses into every facet of the city's political and cultural life. He not only instituted stipends for the poor to serve on juries and to attend the political assembly, but also provided financial support to attend the theater. The common man could, for the first time, cast his vote determining the guilt or innocence of another man, or which policies the city should pursue, or even which tragedy should be awarded first place. In addition to training the masses in naval exercises, Pericles mobilized every craftsman and day laborer in the city by putting them to work in his monumental public works projects. More than simply stuffing their bank accounts, Pericles transformed every individual in the city into creators of awe-inspiring works of beauty. In return for his labors, the common man was promised nothing short of immortality. To magnify the glory of Athens, declares Pericles in his Funeral Oration, is to magnify the glory of its people.

The crimes of Pericles

Pericles was certainly right to recognize the significance of the revolutionary regime that he helped establish. Athenian democracy was not only a model for other Greek city-states, but also serves as an enduring model of self-representative governance throughout the ages. In addition to its revolutionary political constitution, Athens' groundbreaking contributions to nearly every area of artistic and scientific endeavor during its golden age are quite simply astonishing. In spite of its monumental achievements, one cannot ignore the unseemly underbelly that accompanied Athens' emergence as a beacon of liberty. We should, moreover, not be shocked by the ambiguity of Pericles and the regime he founded in light of this philosophic training under Protagoras and other notable sophists.

Protagoras liberated Pericles from the notion that the gods were supervening deities ready to unleash retribution upon acts of injustice. For Protagoras, there is no transcendent standard of justice or injustice beyond what the state determines it to be. Applying Protagoras' relativistic conception of justice, the sophist

Thrasymachus (c. 459–400BC) declares that justice is nothing other than whatever serves "the advantage of the established government" and thus is simply "the advantage of the stronger" (Plato, *Republic* 339a). Armed with this relativistic conception, Pericles could justify what could otherwise be seen as an unjust subjugation of the other cities in the Delian League. Although Plutarch tells us that Pericles never pilfered any money for his personal bank account, he was not beyond misappropriating the funds intended as a means of ensuring the security of the region and spending this money on policies that solely benefitted Athens. Plutarch reports the arguments of Pericles' detractors, who dismissed his various achievements as, in reality, crimes against allied Greek city-states and a disgrace to the Athenian people:

> The people has lost its fair fame and is in ill repute because it has removed the public moneys of the Hellenes from Delos into its own keeping ... of this Pericles has robbed it. And surely Hellas is insulted with a dire insult and manifestly subjected to tyranny when she sees that, with her own enforced contributions for the war, we are gilding and bedizening our city, which, for all the world like a wanton woman, adds to her wardrobe precious stones and costly statues and temples worth their millions. (*Pericles* 12.1–2)

Pericles does not appear to have any misgivings about Athens' unjust actions. We furthermore find the sophistic conception that "might makes right" so engrained in the Athenian political consciousness that they famously defended their subjugation of the city-state of Melos with the declaration that "the strong do what they can and the weak suffer what they must" (Thucydides 5.89).

Plutarch suggests that there were always suspicions that Pericles desired to rule Athens as a tyrant. Protagoras taught Pericles how to realize these aspirations as the wise orator able to impose his will over the masses. Although Pericles never embraced the popular cause in earnest, he understood how winning the favor of the masses would advance his own political career. Plutarch notes how Pericles manipulated the people:

> At this time, therefore, particularly, Pericles gave the reins to the people, and made his policy one of pleasing them, ever devising some sort of a pageant in the town for the masses, or a feast, or a procession, amusing them like children with not uncouth delights. (*Pericles* 11.4)

Protagoras provides not only the first, but one of the most vigorous defenses of self-governance in the history of political thought; nonetheless, his justification of the necessary role of the wise orator in steering the body politic resulted in a tacit form of tyranny.[20] Thucydides famously characterizes the irony of Athenian democracy under Pericles' leadership: "In short, what was nominally a democracy was becoming in his hands government by the first citizen" (Thucydides 2.65).

The various allegations against Pericles caught up with him near the end of his political career. His enemies initially went after his closest associates in a series of criminal trials; they prosecuted his master sculptor Phidias on charges that he embezzled the gold for the statue of Athena, and charged both his concubine Aspasia and his tutor Anaxagoras with impiety. In 430 BC, the public sentiment turned directly against Pericles, holding him responsible for the protracted war with the Spartans and creating the conditions that caused the plague. Not only did they fine him an exorbitant sum, they stripped the respected general and statesman, at least for the time being, of his public office.

Even years after Pericles' death, the Athenians continued to seek retribution against his associates. Around 420 BC, the contempt for Pericles was directed against Protagoras when he was brought up on charges of impiety by the oligarch Pythodorus (Diogenes Laertius 9.8.54).[21] Having been found guilty, a decree was issued to exile him from the city and to burn all copies of his books in the marketplace.

He died shortly thereafter on a sea voyage—possibly in an attempt to
flee Athens. In what must be regarded as some sort of poetic justice,
the father of relativism perished amidst the ceaseless flux of the
crashing seas.

The tragedy of the philosopher-king

It has often been noted that the Greek tragedians drew on the mythic
tradition as a means of cloaking their social commentary about
contemporary political affairs. With this in mind, it may be that the
most famous of all Greek tragedies, *Oedipus Tyrannus*, was meant as
a commentary on the sophistically educated Pericles' rise to power
and his subsequent fall from grace. In the opening lines of the play,
Oedipus is referred to using the phrase *andron de proton* (first among
men). Donald Kagan (1991: 249) notes that Thucydides uses a similar
phrase, *protos aner* ("first man" to refer to Pericles). Building on
Kagan's interpretation, I would note that the first part of Protagoras'
name is spelled out in the phrase. Even more significant in drawing
the connection between Protagoras and the play is the strange means
by which Oedipus assumed the throne of Thebes. Just as Protagoras
renounced the gods and the ancestral tradition, Oedipus murders
both the king of Thebes and his father with a single blow. In a clear
allusion to the devastation the Athenians suffered owing to the
several outbreaks of the plague in the second half of the fifth century,
the Thebans, are also being ravished by a plague. The malevolent
Sphinx vows to lift the plague if someone can solve her vexing riddle:
"What is that which has one voice and yet becomes four-footed and
two-footed and three-footed?" (Apollodorus, *Library* 3.5.8). Nobody
is cunning enough to solve the riddle until Oedipus reveals that the
strange animal that the sphinx has in mind is indeed the human
being, who initially crawls, then walks upright, and finally hobbles

with a walking stick as an elderly man. Oedipus declares that he has solved the riddle solely by the use of his reason and without appeal to the divine signs: "having attained the answer through my wit alone, untaught by birds" (Sophocles, *Oedipus Tyrannus* 370). The Thebans immediately recognize this new kind of savior and appoint him as their philosopher-king. Oedipus assumes the throne and, in his most grave transgression, takes his mother as his wife and queen.

Oedipus' answer to the riddle is a clear allusion to Protagoras' philosophic first principle that the human being is the measure of everything.[22] Like Oedipus, the sophistically trained Pericles represented a wholly new kind of ruler who was granted power to rule the city on account of his wisdom. Although Protagoras' ideas and Pericles' actions liberated Athens' poor from years of subjugation, the injustices perpetuated by the Athenian empire (symbolized by Oedipus' transgressions), reveal the inherent ethical dilemma raised by democratic governance, premised on the principle that the human being is the only arbiter of right and wrong. In the next chapter, I examine Protagoras' ethical ideas with particular focus on his secret teaching.

Protagoras' Secret Teaching

By the Graces! I wonder if Protagoras, who was a very wise man, did not utter this dark saying to the common herd like ourselves, and tell the truth in secret to his pupils.

Socrates in Plato's *Theaetetus* 152c

Protagoras and the history of esotericism

In the previous two chapters, I have respectively detailed Protagoras' rise to fame and fortune as a celebrated teacher of rhetoric and an influential political advisor to Pericles. Up until the point when the Athenians prosecuted him for impiety, Protagoras enjoyed an esteemed reputation throughout his 40-year career. In spite of this, Socrates alleges that the sophist had perpetrated a mass deception this entire time by corrupting his students rather than educating them in virtue (Plato, *Meno* 91d–e; *Protagoras* 313c).[1] Socrates remarks that any other craftsman who defrauded his customers in this way would have quickly gone out of business and starved to death. Even thousands of years later, Protagoras' character remains elusive as equally respected scholars are divided as to whether he should be studied as a foundational thinker in the history of philosophy or dismissed as a charlatan. In this concluding chapter, I attempt to explain what gives rise to such divergent judgments of Protagoras by proposing that he had two sets of instruction: a salutary public teaching that promoted traditional morality and a corrosive private teaching that he revealed to his paying students.

Although the claim that Protagoras had a secret doctrine sounds conspiratorial, it turns out that this practice is not so unusual in the history of philosophy.[2] One should, of course, keep in mind that freedom of speech is a relatively recent political right, which even today is not recognized by many countries around the world.[3] Without this right, individuals risk persecution when voicing ideas that run contrary to their societies' political, religious, and cultural beliefs. This threat poses greater concern for philosophers in light of their systematic attempt to analyze each of these social institutions. As early as the emergence of philosophic speculation, philosophers faced legal threats under the suspicion that they were spreading unorthodox, impious, and subversive ideas to others. It is thus understandable that philosophers facing persecution would employ various ways to conceal controversial ideas while still finding a way to communicate these to their students. In one of the most famous passages documenting the practice, Aristotle reports that Plato taught a different set of ideas in his lectures than in his written works: "It is true, indeed, that the account he gives there of the participant is different from what he says in his so-called unwritten teaching" (*Physics* 209b). Having himself been a student for nearly 20 years at the Academy, Aristotle is certainly a trustworthy witness if Plato had a secret teaching. Furthermore, Plato makes it known in one of his surviving letters that he has serious reservations about committing his ideas to writing: "Every serious man in dealing with really serious subjects carefully avoids writing, lest thereby he may possibly cast them as a prey to the envy and stupidity of the public" (*Epistles* 7.344c). In light of the fate that befell his teacher Socrates, Plato had good reason for being concerned about how his ideas were interpreted by the Athenian public; nonetheless, one is left to wonder why Plato wrote so much when he had such serious reservations about transmitting his ideas in written form.

Although Aristotle indicates that Plato's secret teaching was transmitted orally, he may have also implanted a concealed set of ideas within his written works. Anyone who has spent time with one of Plato's dialogues knows how difficult it is to determine precisely what is being argued. This is further complicated by the fact that many of the dialogues conclude with Socrates declaring that none of the positions that have been examined suffice, and that the issue investigated remains unresolved. In light of this, many first-time readers of the Platonic dialogues are left wondering what Plato's point is in having someone wade through such a difficult argument that concludes without any resolution. Although this is a reasonable response, it is unbelievable that Plato would create these complicated works merely to waste our time. It is much more plausible to assume that Plato is transmitting ideas through the dialogues even though Socrates declares that all the investigated answers are invalid. Furthermore, if we assume that Plato has inserted a secret teaching between the lines of his written works, then we are able to resolve the discrepancy between his aversion to writing and his prodigious output. Employing this peculiar form of writing, Plato could convey his true thoughts within his published works even if they were available for public consumption. At the same time, Plato could safeguard any potentially scandalous ideas from being misapprehended by individuals who were incapable of finding their way through the dialogue's labyrinthine argument.

Having himself been a practitioner of esotericism, Plato provides valuable clues concerning Protagoras' similar attempt to conceal his ideas. The most explicit statement of this is at *Theaetetus* 152c, where Socrates asserts that Protagoras taught different ideas in his public and private lectures.[4] We might further speculate that Protagoras concealed certain ideas within his public teaching that were only detectable by the students enrolled in his private instruction. In the previous chapters, I have significantly drawn upon Plato's *Protagoras*; in this chapter, I return to this dialogue with particular focus on how Protagoras' secret teaching can be unpacked from careful analysis of his public presentation in the "Great Speech."[5] The use of esotericism within this work explains why readers, as well as many scholars, disregard Socrates' judgment and mistakenly interpret Protagoras as a defender of traditional morality.[6]

Before Protagoras is even introduced to the reader first hand, his secret teaching is insinuated through the dialogue's dramatic action. Although older Platonic scholarship tended to disregard the literary elements of the dialogues as mere window dressing, more recent scholarship has come to recognize that the dialogue's dramatic action may be just as important in interpreting the argument as the ideas advanced by the interlocutors. Moreover, it is possible that the dramatic action undermines the explicit argument when one of the interlocutors is shown to be ironic or not completely forthcoming. This repudiation of the explicit argument is precisely what emerges when one is attentive to the dramatic elements in Plato's *Protagoras*.

Plato employs a fairly complicated literary structure in this dialogue by inserting the discussion with Protagoras within the frame of a preliminary dialogue between Socrates and Hippocrates, and a second frame in which Socrates recounts the entire discussion later in the day to an unnamed friend. These multiple layers of discussion inset within one another mirror the levels of disclosure that distinguish an initiate of Protagoras' secret teaching from someone simply attending one of his public lectures. The theme of concealment and disclosure is signaled with the dialogue's opening line in which the unnamed friend presses Socrates to reveal the intimate details of his amorous relationship with his young lover Alcibiades. With seeming allusion to exoteric and esoteric kinds of knowledge, Socrates redirects the conversation by affirming to the friend that the internal beauty of Protagoras' mind was more captivating to him than the external beauty of Alcibiades' body (309c). The beauty of a mind is, of course, fundamentally different from the beauty of a body, and this distinction mirrors the similar divide between the outer and inner meaning of an argument. Just as we can be charmed by someone's appearance, so too can we be seduced by a persuasive speech.[7] Prior to meeting Protagoras, Socrates warns his friend Hippocrates that the sophist's doctrines will poison his mind quicker than he can assess their merits (314b). Socrates returns to this analogy after Protagoras has concluded his speech by affirming that just as a physician cannot determine a patient's health without having him strip bare, so too can the meaning of an argument not be assessed solely by considering its surface layer. He thus beckons Protagoras to expose his true ideas beneath the surface of his public teaching: "Come, my good Protagoras, uncover some more of your thoughts" (352a).

Prior to Protagoras' presentation of the "Great Speech," he is depicted delivering a private lecture to his students. The entire scene is cast like an initiation rite into one of the ancient mystery cults. In an absolute state of frenzy, Hippocrates comes to Socrates in the middle of the night soliciting his help as an intercessor in order to become one of Protagoras' private students (310c). Assuring Hippocrates that he knows where to find Protagoras, Socrates reveals that the sophist most known for his outspokenness, is actually a quite secretive individual who prefers to spend the majority of his time indoors (311a). This sense of seclusion is further stressed when Socrates and Hippocrates are initially barred entrance to the house where Protagoras is giving his lectures (314d). Despite his later declaration to practice sophistry publically (317b), Protagoras' true teaching is literally concealed behind closed doors. Interestingly, the safeguarding of Protagoras' wisdom foreshadows Zeus' similar safeguarding of political wisdom within the mythic section of the "Great Speech" (321d). As I will later argue, this minor narrative detail holds the key for interpreting the myth and unlocking Protagoras' secret teaching.

When Socrates is finally granted entrance and encounters the
elusive Protagoras for the first time, he compares Protagoras to the
semi-divine poet Orpheus (315a). The cultic atmosphere of the scene
is further reinforced as some in attendance are found, of all things,
dancing during Protagoras' lecture (315b). In addition to these less
attentive observers, Socrates describes two distinct groups of students
who trail Protagoras in a ritualistic manner:

> It was fine to see the orderly manner in which his train of listeners
> split up into two parties on this side and on that, and wheeling round
> formed up again each time in his rear most admirably. (315b)

In addition to this core group of students, there is a gathering of
individuals outside of the circle who only hear bits and pieces
of Protagoras' lecture, though are nonetheless charmed by his
words. Despite being cautious about attributing a secret teaching to
Protagoras, the esteemed Plato scholar James Adam interprets the
symbolism of these individuals as representative of the exoteric and
esoteric levels on which the sophist's lecture can be apprehended:
"there is an allusion to an outer circle of Protagorean students, deemed
unworthy of the subtlest teaching of the master" (1905: 94). Socrates
then approaches Protagoras and informs him that Hippocrates
wishes to be one of his students; however, Protagoras wants clari-
fication whether Hippocrates desires private or public instruction,
cautioning him that there are consequences to entering his inner
circle (316b–d).

Having alluded to Protagoras' public and private teachings, Plato
now makes esotericism an explicit theme of the dialogue as he has
Protagoras deliver a disquisition on the history of this practice. In
one of the most provocative claims in the history of Western literature, Protagoras asserts that nearly all of the most influential figures
responsible for shaping Greek culture have practiced esotericism
by concealing their potentially scandalous ideas under the guise of

a salutary public teaching. He identifies these thinkers as sophists and thus associates the fifth-century movement of itinerant teachers of morality and rhetoric with this ancient tradition of esotericism: "Now I tell you that sophistry is an ancient art, and those men of ancient times who practised it, fearing the odium it involved, disguised it in a decent dress" (316d). Protagoras goes on to identify nine specific individuals that were a part of this clandestine tradition of sophistry. Laurence Lampert comments on Protagoras' catalogue of concealed sophists: "his list is anything but haphazard for it includes the chief elements of Greek education—poetry, religion, gymnastic, and music—and some of the most honored names" (2010: 38).

Protagoras' claim about the practice of concealed sophistry is nothing short of a wholesale indictment of Greek culture. The most troubling of his various allegations is the charge that the mystics and poets may have used religion as a means of disguising their ulterior motives. Although Protagoras does not provide specifics regarding exactly what any of these individuals were concealing in their public teaching, we might speculate that he is attributing to them the same ideas that he professes publically as an avowed sophist. It is certainly plausible that others prior to Protagoras have questioned the existence of the gods and concluded that human beings are the only measure of truth. Although Protagoras' ennobling of human beings may not in itself seem scandalous, Socrates alleges that the secret doctrine behind the human-measure fragment affirms that there is no claim to any reality beyond our ceaseless and fleeting perceptions of the world (Plato, *Theaetetus* 152d). With allusion to Protagoras' claim regarding the history of concealed sophists, Socrates further charges that nearly every poet and philosopher has secretly held the position of ontological and epistemological relativism (Plato, *Theaetetus* 152e).

If Protagoras' and Socrates' views about the poets are correct, then we are left with the scandalous conclusion that these esteemed individuals may not have believed in any transcendent truth, let alone the gods that animate their tales.[8] A little later in the dialogue, Protagoras provides the following claim about the value of a critical reading of the poets:

> The greatest part of a man's education is to be skilled in the matter of verse; that is, to be able to apprehend, in the utterances of the poets, what has been rightly and what wrongly composed, and to know how to distinguish them and account for them when questioned (339a).

At first glance, Protagoras' insistence on the close study of poetry as the foundation of education seems to support traditional Greek values. For hundreds of years, the works of Homer and Hesiod were believed to provide a faithful account of the cosmic order and were thus employed as the primary means of inculcating the young in the religious, ethical, and cultural values of Greek society. A critical analysis of poetic works would therefore seem to be a noble and pious endeavor, even if this entails, as Protagoras prescribes, correcting anything that has been "wrongly composed." Notwithstanding the great reverence the Greeks had for Homer, would it not be important to correct a misstatement found in his works when this involves matters of the greatest significance?

We are fortunate to have several examples of Protagoras' critical analysis of Homer's poetry. Two of these examples concern the most famous line of all Greek literature: the opening invocation of the muse in Homer's *Iliad*. The line reads in the original Greek: "Mēnin aeide thea Pēlēiadeō Akhileōs oulomenēn" (Rage, sing Goddess of Peleus' son Achilles' destructive rage) (Homer, *Iliad* 1.1).[9] The very first word of the poem does not escape Protagoras' scrutiny as he charges that *menis* (rage), which is grammatically feminine, should more properly be classified as a masculine noun and it, therefore, follows that the modifying adjective, *oulomenēn* (destructive), should take a masculine form (Aristotle, *On Sophistical Refutations* 173b). Beyond making a simple grammar mistake, Protagoras insinuates that Homer should be taken to task for expressing the wrath of the greatest of the Greek heroes as a feminine attribute.[10] Protagoras additionally chastises the poet for having committed a much graver indiscretion by commanding the muse using an imperative form *aeide thea* (sing goddess) rather than supplicating himself by using the optative form of the verb (Aristotle, *Poetics* 1456b). Despite Protagoras' pious pretentions, Aristotle (who is himself known for drawing subtle distinctions), dismisses the sophist's criticism of Homer as nothing more than semantic quibbling: "The knowledge or ignorance of such matters brings upon the poet no censure worth serious consideration" (*Poetics* 1456b).

Although Protagoras' demand for linguistic precision does not constitute a serious critique of Homer, his allegations in Plato's dialogue regarding the entire poetic and cultural tradition is, on the contrary, quite serious. Is Protagoras the first individual to have questioned the existence of the gods, or is he simply the first individual to have admitted this publicly? Moreover, just as the agnostic Protagoras employs the gods of mythology in his public teaching, so too might other shrewd individuals realize the value of promulgating religion, even when they themselves do not necessarily believe in the gods. Employing this sort of noble lie, political leaders can appeal to religion to provide divine sanctioning for various ethical precepts that they wish to promote.

Although Protagoras' claim about previous educators invites an interesting direction for speculation, we must ultimately leave unsettled whether or not this is simply an attempt to have his own motives seem less subversive. In a famous series of lectures about the role of religion in early Greek philosophy, Werner Jaeger brought attention to Protagoras' understanding of the value of religion for politics.[11] Drawing on Jaeger's work, Laurence Lampert remarks on Protagoras' use of civic religion in the "Great Speech":

> Protagoras is not just enlightened about religion and its human sources; he aspires to use religion to advance enlightenment by civilizing and tempering the religion of the vast majority who would not be well served by being enlightened about religion. Civil gods could serve a civil order, promoting justice and moderation among the many who notice almost nothing but merely repeat whatever their leaders proclaim. (2010: 60)

As I have discussed in the previous chapter, Protagoras defends democracy as the best regime. This is premised on the recognition that all human beings are valid judges of right and wrong. While legitimizing the thoughts and opinions of the masses, Protagoras also establishes the essential role of the wise orator in helping to shape public opinion through the art of rhetoric and persuasion. Lampert's understanding of Protagoras' use of civic religion exposes a crack in the seeming harmony between the wise orator and the populace. On the one hand, religion serves a salutary function in establishing a transcendent basis of justice. On the other hand, Protagoras' appeal to the gods in the "Great Speech," despite his uncertainty of their existence, suggests how the wise orator can employ noble lies to manipulate the masses. As Lampert notes, this situates the leader in a morally ambiguous position outside of the juridical system that he helps establish.[12] With this understanding of politics in mind, I now turn to an interpretation of the public and private teaching of Protagoras' "Great Speech."

Esotericism in the "Great Speech"

Before embarking on the "Great Speech," Protagoras queries the audience whether they would rather hear his argument in the form of a fable or a philosophical discourse (320c). Since those in attendance leave the decision up to him, he decides on the fable as the more appealing way to express his ideas. Several implications follow from Protagoras' seemingly arbitrary decision. Obviously, a fable will be more accessible and more entertaining than a logical argument, and thus reach a much wider audience. The teller of the tale merely needs to persuade his audience of the intended moral without having to prove its validity. The most significant advantage that Protagoras gains by delivering his teaching in the form of a myth is the inherent ambiguity of interpreting a story's meaning. This results in individuals deriving radically different interpretations from the same narrative elements. Playing off this ambiguity, Protagoras is able to employ the myth so as to convey both a moralistic public teaching, as well as an immoral secret doctrine. The factor determining which of these two interpretations the individual will derive is the respective world view that he brings to the interpretive activity. For most of Protagoras' audience, we can assume that this would mean an orthodox devotion to the traditional religious, ethical, and cultural beliefs upheld by Greek society. These individuals would, moreover, immediately associate Protagoras' appeal to the traditional myths about the gods as identifying him as a fellow practitioner of traditional religion and as a trustworthy spokesman on the subject of morality. Aristotle notes how the speaker's ability to win the audience's trust can help in persuading them of the argument: "But as proofs are established not only by demonstrative, but also by ethical argument—since we have confidence in an orator who exhibits certain qualities, such as goodness, good will or both …" (*Rhetoric* 1366a). The more a speaker is able to establish his good character in the minds of his audience, the more they will be disposed to ignore inconsistencies in his speech that might otherwise be perceived as promoting immorality.

Although Protagoras could win over and persuade the majority of his audience with his pious pretentions, his private students would be able to see past the rhetoric of his public lectures to grasp its encoded message. In this regard, one should keep in mind that Protagoras was delivering a private lecture before Socrates and Hippocrates arrived at the house of Callias. It should further be noted that while Protagoras was certainly paid by Callias, no money changed hands after Socrates' arrival. Moreover, Protagoras only broaches the issue of being compensated after he has concluded the "Great Speech." Since Protagoras is such a strong proponent of intellectual property, it is safe to assume that he would not give away his knowledge without money changing hands. Although Socrates and Hippocrates remain in the dark regarding the contents of the private session, we can assume that some of the wiser students of the private lecture would be able to apply what they learned to the "Great Speech." As previously discussed, even Protagoras' private instruction was apprehended at several different levels: the dancers who are completely oblivious to his lecture, the outer circle that are charmed by his words without a full understanding of its meaning, and the two groups of students that are a part of Protagoras' inner circle. Additionally, Socrates reveals that one individual within the inner circle of students is taking the course professionally under Protagoras with the aim of becoming a sophist (315a). Besides Protagoras himself, we can assume that this single individual, Antimoerus of Mende, is the one best equipped to offer a thorough analysis of the meaning of the myth. Unfortunately, we do not know anything else about Antimoerus and are thus left to uncover the myth's secret teaching on our own.

Protagoras never reveals (as one might expect), the source of the myth he recounts, leaving us to conclude that it was largely of his own devising. Although he does draw on the commonly accepted tradition regarding Prometheus role in the creation of man, he significantly recasts elements of the story to suit his political agenda. The most striking implication of this revision is how he is able to draw on the mythic tradition, which has always served to legitimate monarchy and a rigid notion of social stratification, to defend and promote governance predicated on the universality of virtue and the equality of all people. The myth further attempts to rejuvenate the role of the gods within democracy in spite of Protagoras' precept that the human being is the only measure of truth. That said, we must recognize the obvious irony of his appeals to both the gods and the traditional stories about them in light of his staunch skepticism about their existence and his practice of not appealing to the gods in his teaching: "You bring in the gods, the question of whose existence or non-existence I exclude from oral and written discussion" (Plato, *Theaetetus* 162d). Although it appears that Protagoras has violated his basic epistemological and methodological principles in the myth he recounts, we are able to resolve this contradiction if we assume that he is employing esotericism in the "Great Speech," and thus is conveying conflicting messages in its inner and outer layers.[13] Despite his claim to be different from the concealed sophists in openly admitting his practice of the sophistic art, Protagoras similarly employed a public teaching as an "outer covering" to disguise a more subversive private teaching (317a).[14]

In what follows, I summarize the details of the myth as they are intended to be interpreted by those uninitiated in Protagoras' secret teaching. After establishing Protagoras' public teaching, I then show how inconsistencies within the myth reveal his secret doctrine.

The public teaching of Protagoras' "Great Speech"

Protagoras begins his fable by considering a time prior to the creation of mortal creatures when only the gods existed. Immediately, this establishes the gods' supremacy over all other beings. After the gods had formed each of the living creatures in the womb of the earth, they charged the Titan deities, Epimetheus and Prometheus, with the task of providing each beast with a faculty that would ensure its survival. Having carelessly distributed various physical attributes to each of the animal species, Epimetheus realized that there was no trait remaining to ensure the survival of humankind. Without some sort of protective endowment, humans remained in a state of utter helplessness: "Man was naked, unshod, unbedded, unarmed" (321c). Disturbed by Epimetheus' absent-mindedness in caring for the human species, Prometheus took matters into his own hands. Although all the physical attributes had been distributed, Prometheus bequeathed the divinely held knowledge of fire and the productive arts to humans so as to ensure their intellectual superiority over the other beasts. The initial impulse of the primal individuals was to employ their newly acquired wisdom to worship the gods by erecting altars and fashioning idols (322a). Only after subordinating themselves before the divine did individuals apply their newly obtained gifts to secure their survival by developing various arts aimed at providing them with food, clothing, and shelter. Despite the many advantages afforded by the development of these arts, the primal individuals of the myth remained in a state of incapacity owing to their inability to perform collective action. Since a ferocious animal could easily overtake a single individual even if he should be furnished with arms, the viability of the human race remained precarious without the ability to act collectively. This urgent crisis resulted in the founding of the first cities. Although these early associations provided protection against the wild beasts, individuals now found themselves in conflict with one another as they competed for scarce resources within the city (322b). Fearing that this internecine strife would be the destruction of the human race, Zeus could no longer sit idly by and charged the messenger god Hermes with the task of bestowing humans with political wisdom so that people could live together in harmony. Since communities rely on particular individuals to provide services to the city based on their expertise, Hermes asks whether Zeus would like him to distribute political knowledge to only a few specialists or to everyone within the city. Zeus clarifies Hermes' mission by proclaiming that, unlike craft knowledge, the salvation of civic life depends on all individuals possessing an understanding of ethics.

> Let all have their share: for cities cannot be formed if only a few have a share of these as of other arts. And make thereto a law of my ordaining, that he who cannot partake of respect and right shall die the death as a public pest. (322d)

Although Zeus has always been the deity responsible for upholding justice, Protagoras has masterfully redefined the god's role from the paradigmatic monarch to the founder of democratic governance. Whereas classical mythology celebrated a race of heroes possessing superior virtue, Protagoras' myth has established, with Zeus' sanctioning, justice and virtue as universal qualities that are capable of being possessed by all human beings. Even as late as the fifth century, there persisted a rigid notion of social stratification that classified individuals according to their family lineage as either noble (*agathoi*) or baseborn (*kakoi*). Protagoras' myth is an attempt to constitute a new conception of anthropology that assumes, at least in terms of capacity, the equality of all individuals.

Protagoras follows his retelling of the myth by providing a logical explanation of its moral teaching. Despite employing reason in this section of the "Great Speech," we should nonetheless regard it as a part of the same public teaching as the mythic section since his explicit aim is simply to justify the myth's central doctrine by appealing to commonly held opinions about ethics. In this regard, he notes that public sentiment regarding the universality of virtue is so strong that there is an expectation that even the most wicked individual should profess his righteousness in public: "Everyone, they say, should profess to be just, whether he is so or not, and whoever does not make some pretension to justice is mad" (323b). Even the scoundrel recognizes that he ought to act ethically, and thus realizes the social expectation that he declare his righteousness.

Although Protagoras establishes that all individuals have a capacity for virtue, he contends that this potential is only realized through "application and learning" (324a). He thus argues that virtue is acquired in a similar manner as one might learn technical knowledge.[15] This helps clarify an important point raised in the myth regarding exactly what Prometheus had bequeathed to humanity. Obviously, individuals are not born with the specific principles that underlie each of the productive arts implanted in their souls, but merely the cognitive capacity for understanding and utilizing them. Although it is obvious that technical knowledge is acquired through instruction and practice, Greek society maintained the prejudicial notion that a disposition for ethical action was an inheritable trait based on one's lineage. Once again, Protagoras grounds his claim about the role of nurture in instilling virtue by appealing to social practice, noting that individuals would not scrutinize their neighbor's ethical conduct if virtue were an inborn trait. Furthermore, he argues that society punishes wrongdoers not out of vengeance for past actions, but rather with an eye to rehabilitating the offender (324b–c). He builds on this claim by detailing the extensive socialization process beginning with the parents' instruction of the infant and continuing in a seemingly unbroken chain as they hand over this responsibility to tutors, schoolmasters, trainers, and finally the city's lawmakers. Each of these teachers of virtue employs the same paradigmatic model for instilling ethical conduct:

> and as each act and word occurs they teach and impress upon him that this is just, and that unjust, one thing noble, another base, one holy, another unholy, and that he is to do this, and not do that. If he readily

obeys,—so; but if not, they treat him as a bent and twisted piece of wood and straighten him with threats and blows. (325d)

Given that every cultural and political institution in Greek society is dedicated to the sole purpose of instilling ethics in individuals, Protagoras seems to have provided overwhelming evidence to support the notion that virtue can be taught and that all are capable of learning it. Having established this, Protagoras is left to explain why some individuals fail to act ethically if morality is indeed a teachable subject. Protagoras answers this vexing question by drawing on an analogy between developing a moral disposition and acquiring knowledge of a technical subject. As discussed extensively in the previous chapter, he illustrates the point by imagining a society that dedicates as much effort to training its citizens to play an instrument as traditional Greek societies dedicate to learning ethics, and concludes that these efforts would similarly result in a wide range of musical abilities. Rather than undermining the claim that virtue can be taught, the recalcitrant student substantiates that morality is teachable insofar as the educational process reveals a range of learners.

Protagoras concludes the "Great Speech" by presenting himself as simply another in a long line of teachers sanctioned by Greek society to instruct the young in virtue. He thereby completes his public instruction with a sales pitch for interested students to seek him out for his private instruction:

If there is somebody who excels us ever so little in showing the way to virtue, we must be thankful. Such an one I take myself to be, excelling all other men in the gift of assisting people to become good and true, and giving full value for the fee that I charge. (328a–b)

It is quite understandable how anyone in the audience during Protagoras' "Great Speech" might come away with the impression that he is an exemplary teacher of morality. Rather than promoting any sort of subversive teaching, Protagoras has grounded his ideas in the long-held stories and beliefs about the gods and their respective role in human affairs. Moreover, he backs up his fable by appealing to all of the traditional cultural and political institutions. Even his boastful claim to be the preeminent teacher of ethics can be excused for its admirable intentions.

The secret teaching of Protagoras' "Great Speech"

Notwithstanding Protagoras' pious pretentions, it is hard to ignore his warning that sophists throughout history have employed moralistic guises to conceal their subversive ideas. Of course, Protagoras claims to be different than these secretive sophists since he publically acknowledges that he practices sophistry, and thus has nothing to hide (317b–c). Although this leads us to take him at his word, we must consider that his professed honesty is simply another means of subterfuge. In addition, he tells us, in all candor, that an immoral man would never be truthful about his immorality unless he was mad. Why should we then trust his self-professed claim to be the world's preeminent teacher of morality when he informs us that he would not be so foolish as to admit that, in reality, he promotes anything but what he claims? Let us then re-examine the "Great Speech," attempting to read between the lines and piece together its secret teaching.

Protagoras is known for having ennobled humans by repositioning their place in the universe as the ultimate arbiters of truth. In spite of this, the myth treats humans as simply another species in the animal kingdom whose primary motivation is survival. This primal instinct for survival remains intact despite the several transformations that early humans undergo as they form social bonds and develop various arts and sciences. In this regard, it should be noted that the myth asserts that humans come to identify their superiority over the other animals as a result of being the sole creature possessing intelligence (322a). That said, the ascendancy of primal humans over the rest of the animal world amounts to nothing more than their ability to utilize knowledge to preserve their existence.

Prior to the founding of the first cities, the primal individuals are portrayed within the myth as having no innate inclination to forge social bonds. Moreover, when individuals established the first alliances, it is not out of any sort of altruistic motives, but rather out of a self-interested need to wage war against wild animals that are too ferocious to subdue individually. Protagoras recounts this self-serving motive behind the first social alliances:

> Although their skill in handiwork was a sufficient aid in respect of food, in their warfare with the beasts it was defective; for as yet they had no civic art, which includes the art of war. So they sought to band themselves together and secure their lives by founding cities. (322b)

It is clear that Protagoras understands social solidarity as nothing more than an alliance of self-interested actors working together against a common enemy.[16] Since individuals within the fledgling cities had no instinctual concern for the common good and had no compunction against wronging one another, the viability of these associations was tenuous at best (322b). Just as cooperative action emerged out of the need to declare war against the wild beast; political wisdom arose as a means of subduing vicious individuals fighting in a war of all against all within the city.

Although the myth primarily understands human action as motivated by the need to ensure one's survival, it should be noted that it does, ever so briefly, reference some activities that do not seem to have utilitarian ends. Even before applying the knowledge of the arts to any practical use, Protagoras informs us that the first impulse of the primal individuals was to worship the gods by constructing altars and fashioning idols (322a). Our ultimate judgment of the myth depends on precisely how we interpret this minor detail. We might conclude that Protagoras is acknowledging two of the most important activities in distinguishing human beings from the rest of the animal kingdom: a religious inclination to seek for the divine and a creative impulse expressed through the production of works of art. Moreover, he appears to grant these non-instrumental activities more primacy than the instinct for survival since they are acknowledged as the first activities humans pursued after having acquired knowledge of the arts.

Although the religious and aesthetic realms represent a more exultant conception of humanity than beasts fighting for survival, Protagoras does not pursue this line of thought in the rest of the "Great Speech." On the contrary, he tells us that the impulse to celebrate the gods was motivated by primal humans realizing their own godlike status as fellow possessors of knowledge (322a). Drozdek (2005: 44) thus imagines that these statues honoring the gods were made in the image of humans. Rather than recognizing the human ability to commune with a transcendent realm, the construction of altars and the fashioning of statues represent a celebration of humankind and its ascendancy over the other species. Despite its religious overtones, the construction of statues serves as an instantiation of Protagoras' fundamental principle that the human being is, in reality, the only measure of all things. Read in the context of the myth, the significance of his aphorism is simply that intelligence affords the human race with a greater ability for survival than any of the other species in the animal kingdom.

Since the primal humans of the myth consider themselves to have a kinship with the divine, it is imperative to understand precisely how the myth is conceiving of the gods. As has been noted, Protagoras' appeal to the gods as upholding civic justice establishes him in the minds of the uninitiated as a defender of traditional religion and morality. A closer analysis of the actions of the gods within the myth, however, reveals his sacrilegious and immoral views. Despite the myth's overt appeal to the gods in shaping the development of the created world, Protagoras presents us with an early formulation of a natural ecosystem that is regulated by the ability of each species to survive rather than by any sort of divine oversight.[17] As discussed in a previous chapter, Greek mythology understands the gods as the natural forces underlying the cosmic order. This allows agnostic Protagoras to draw on the traditional gods without violating his skepticism about their existence. Although the public teaching of the myth stresses the gods' concern for the human race, one should note that these acts of divine agency are, in reality, compensation after the fact for the gods' complete disregard for the welfare of humankind. The lack of concern on the part of Epimetheus is, of course, an explicit theme of the myth, which initially leads us to believe that he alone, among the immortal deities, is to blame for the deficiencies of the human race. After closer consideration of the myth, it is obvious that the other gods, with the sole exception of Prometheus, were equally without concern for the fate of mankind. One should keep in mind that the gifts of Athena and Hephaestus were not given willingly to humankind, but were only obtained through Prometheus' deception—an act for which Protagoras reminds us he would later be punished (322a). If the gods truly have humans' best interests in mind, then why would they have punished Prometheus for his well-intentioned intervention on behalf of the human race? Like the other Olympians, Zeus should also be held accountable for his indifference to the plight of humankind. Not only does he initially withhold the knowledge of civic justice, he prevents anyone from obtaining access to it by securing it behind the walls of his well-guarded citadel. Once again, one wonders why Zeus would go to such extreme measures to keep political knowledge out of the hands of mortals if he truly had concern for their wellbeing. Although the

entire myth culminates with Zeus' dramatic entrance into human
affairs, it is obvious from Protagoras' analysis that the divine gift
of political wisdom is worthless without the extensive socialization
process.

Protagoras identifies three cardinal virtues as constituting the
totality of human virtue: moderation, justice, and holiness (325a).
Although one would expect that the stories he tells about the
gods would help to inculcate ethics by providing his audience with
moral exemplars of these traits, Protagoras' gods violate each of his
cardinal virtues. This begins with Epimetheus' thoughtless immod-
eration, described by Protagoras as having "heedlessly squandered
his stock of properties on the brutes ..." (321c). The consequences
of Epimetheus' immoderate behavior are further compounded by
the injustice committed by Athena, Hephaestus, and Zeus, who each
withhold knowledge from humankind that is vital to their survival.[18]
Zeus' violation of justice is even more problematic than the other
gods' transgressions since it is his role to ensure that this virtue
is upheld by others. Moreover, while the other gods have merely
committed an act of omission by failing to render to the mortals
what is owed them, Zeus actively prevents mortals from obtaining
civic wisdom by safeguarding it behind the walls of his well-protected
citadel. The obvious lesson of the gods' hypocrisy is that they are
beyond the law that they mandate for others. The implications of this
for actual politics are pursued by the sophist Thrasymachus, who
cynically observes that the ruling party in all regimes establishes laws
that are to the detriment of those who must obey them, but to the
advantage of those in power (Plato, *Republic* 338e). For this reason,
Thrasymachus contends that injustice is more advantageous than
justice when one is able to rule the city as a tyrant (Plato, *Republic*
344a).

The series of divine transgressions detailed in the myth culminate
in Prometheus' even more egregious act of injustice in which he steals

from the other gods. As the god that takes the greatest interest in the welfare of humankind, Prometheus initially appears to be the hero of the tale. He is, nonetheless, an ambiguous character who is both celebrated and censured for his misdeed. On the one hand, his crime is a clear violation of standards of justice and piety. On the other hand, his forethought and boldness ensure the survival of the human race in the face of continuous threats posed by the natural world. In spite of his obvious transgressions, Prometheus exhibits two of the most important virtues. Curiously, Protagoras forgot to mention these moral ideals when providing what he claimed to be an exhaustive list of human virtues at 325a. This oversight does not escape Socrates, who later interrogates Protagoras as to whether he considers wisdom and courage to be virtues (330a). Despite having failed to mention them earlier, Protagoras now affirms that these certainly are virtues, and that wisdom should be regarded as the preeminent virtue. Any careful reader should be asking how Protagoras so carelessly forgot these two virtues when he now recognizes their primacy. At least one scholar finds this to be no absent-minded omission on the part of Protagoras, but rather a deliberate attempt to define two distinct ethical systems. Hemmenway clarifies Protagoras' conception of demotic and elite ethics, which correlate with the myth's public and private teaching:

> Demotic virtue, mainly for the many, is simple-minded restraint and law-abidingness. It produces civil order and is primarily associated with the cardinal virtues of moderation and justice. Elite virtue, for the few, consists of daring and cleverness. It is the instrument of political success and it is primarily associated with courage and wisdom. (1996: 2)

Protagoras not only presents these two ethical systems in the myth, but also demonstrates their opposing imperatives with the story of Prometheus' noble act of injustice. Moreover, when pressed by Socrates, Protagoras openly acknowledges this contradiction:

"many are brave but unjust, and many again are just but not wise" (329e).

Although Protagoras reminds us that Prometheus was punished for his crime, it is interesting that the gods never rebuke humans for availing themselves of the fruits of his ill-gotten gain. On the contrary, the salvation of the human race depends on individuals utilizing the stolen knowledge of the arts to provide themselves with food, clothing, and shelter. Rather than grounding the universality of ethics, the necessity of using stolen property establishes the primacy of the survival instinct in humans over any innate ethical imperative. Despite purporting that the myth will prove that justice is an inborn trait, Protagoras affirms just after concluding the myth that this sort of knowledge is not "natural or spontaneous, but as something taught and acquired after careful preparation by those who acquire it" (323c). He then details the extensive socialization process that attempts to civilize the bestial nature of humans. Society literally beats justice into individuals to counter their natural orientation to pursue injustice. Any parent can attest to the fact that children have a natural disposition to act selfishly. While the child needs no instruction to learn how to pursue his own interest, endless effort is extended to inculcate the child with a concern for others. The persistent need to monitor individuals' actions throughout the entirety of their lives confirms that individuals never come to accept that justice is in itself beneficial. The educational system merely reinforces that there are rewards and punishments for one's actions when perceived by others. The only reason to act ethically is therefore to reap the rewards and avoid the punishments. That said, the ethical action remains a violation of basic human nature in which the individual knows that he can often derive much greater rewards from acting unjustly if his misdeeds go undetected.[19] Despite the social stigma associated with injustice, everyone would admit—if being honest—that injustice is more profitable than justice. Willing to articulate this view publically, Thrasymachus unapologetically declares, "the unjust is what profits man's self and is for his advantage" (Plato, *Republic* 344c).

In spite of the need for inculcating ethics through the socialization process, defenders of morality might still argue that ethical precepts are universal. Protagoras undermines this argument with his understanding of the acquisition of ethics as analogous to learning something as random as being able to play the flute. He claims that ethical instruction is so alien to the individual that the wickedest individual in a civilized society would be regarded as a model of virtue and justice if compared to someone who did not receive ethical instruction:

> You must regard any man who appears to you the most unjust person ever reared among human laws and society as a just man and a craftsman of justice, if he had to stand comparison with people who lacked education and law courts and laws and any constant compulsion to the pursuit of virtue. (327c–d)

If morality were somehow universal, would not any person regardless of his upbringing have access to ethical precepts, even if these had not been cultivated through habituation and practice? At most, we can conclude that people are born with a capacity to adopt ethical norms, but no innate disposition to act in a specific way. In this regard, acquiring ethical precepts is similar to language acquisition. Human beings are hardwired with a capacity to communicate, but we are not born with knowledge of any specific language. Our mother tongue is solely determined by the linguistic community in which we are raised.

If indeed ethics is similar to language acquisition, then our belief system is as arbitrary as the ethical community in which we are acculturated. Although we may want to believe that our political, ethical, and religious beliefs have transcendent truth, we must consider whether we would hold the same beliefs if we were raised in a culture with a different value system. This leads us to consider whether there are more similarities or differences between cultures. We might still argue for ethical universals if cultures have different practices to express the same universal principle. This would be comparable to languages employing different words to express the same referent. In contrast, one might argue that each particular linguistic system is fundamentally constitutive of meaning, and that no universal referent exists outside of the prison house of language. This issue is investigated by one of Protagoras' disciples in an anonymous fourth-century work known as the *Dissoi Logoi* (Contrasting Arguments).[20] The author examines, through a comparison of different cultural practices, whether the same things are universally regarded as respectable or shameful. Through this empirical research of actual practices, we can see that cultures not only have trivial differences, but have contrasting beliefs about whether things like cannibalism, incest, and pederasty are noble or base (*Dissoi Logoi* 2.9–17). In one of the most shocking of these various cultural practices, the author reports, "The Massagetes cut up their parents and eat them, and they think that to be buried in their children is the most beautiful grave imaginable" (*Dissoi Logoi* 2.14). He then poses a thought experiment in which every nation in the world places something that their culture found disgraceful onto a heap and then in turn takes something from the heap left by another nation that their culture found noble, and concludes that nothing would remain since there are no ethical absolutes (*Dissoi Logoi* 2.18).

The cross-cultural analysis conducted by the author of the *Dissoi Logoi* reveals the fundamental tension inherent in Protagoras' human-measure maxim. The divergent examples of cultural practices suggest that the community is the only measure of truth that is available to most individuals; however, the individual who is able to achieve objectivity in viewing these divergent practices recognizes that there is no ultimate truth concerning human affairs. It is this renunciation of transcendent ethical precepts that leads the sophistically enlightened student to the realization that, in the final analysis, the individual is the only valid arbiter of truth. Moreover, since the restrictions regulating justice and holiness are merely arbitrary, why should the individual not transgress the law when he knows he can reap greater rewards by acting unjustly?

Protagorean virtue

Although Prometheus initially appears as the hero of the myth, he ultimately pays the penalty for his crimes. His punishment consequently serves as a valuable reminder that unjust actions have consequences when detected by others. It is for this reason that Thrasymachus dismisses the petty criminal: "For each several part of such wrongdoing the malefactor who fails to escape detection is fined and incurs the extreme of contumely; for temple-robbers, kidnappers, burglars, swindlers, and thieves the appellations of those who commit these partial forms of injustice" (Plato, *Republic* 344b). Protagoras' appeal to punishment as a tool for teaching virtue only ends up reinforcing the notion that there are consequences to getting caught, and not that there is anything inherently wrong with the illicit behavior. The individual thus learns to be deceptive enough to pursue his natural inclination for injustice without being detected. In his famous thought experiment in which just and unjust individuals were given a magical ring with the power to make one invisible, Glaucon argues that both would similarly commit illicit acts knowing that there would not be any repercussions (Plato, *Republic* 359c). Although the practicality of Glaucon's experiment may seem farfetched, Protagoras notes that even the simplest person recognizes the value of rhetoric for manipulating how others perceive one's actions (323b). Beyond merely engendering a good reputation, Protagoras promises to teach his students how to become such adept rhetoricians that they can make the weaker speech defeat the stronger, and thus avoid the consequences of unjust actions if their injustice should be detected.

Although the petty thief demonstrates boldness in his willingness to commit an illicit act, his likelihood of getting caught and paying the price for his unjust actions shows his lack of wisdom. Despite his momentary victory, Prometheus is shown to be just as foolish as his brother Epimetheus. Not only was his misdeed ultimately detected, but Protagoras tells us that he was not clever enough in his stealth to have sufficiently provided the human race with what it needed to secure its wellbeing:

> Now although man acquired in this way the wisdom of daily life, civic wisdom he had not, since this was in the possession of Zeus; Prometheus could not make so free as to enter the citadel which is the dwelling-place of Zeus, and moreover the guards of Zeus were terrible: but he entered unobserved the building shared by Athena and Hephaestus ... (321d)

Protagoras suggests that there would have been no need for Zeus' intervention in human affairs if Prometheus were a more adept thief, able to evade Zeus' guards and penetrate his citadel.

Having exposed Prometheus as a failed messiah, Protagoras reveals Zeus as the true savior of mankind. Zeus, the paradigmatic monarch, is refashioned from his former role in sanctioning monarchic government to his new role as the founder of a regime premised on the equality of all citizens. Just as Solon, and later Pericles, had ended the class warfare by instituting democratic reforms, Zeus resolves the civic strife by empowering all citizens as enforcers of the law. That said, Zeus stands outside of the system that he institutes and therefore is able to transgress justice without suffering any repercussions. Protagoras upholds Zeus, in his role as statesman and founder of democracy, as the ultimate moral exemplar. We are now able to understand Protagoras' promise to his potential students that their private interests will best be served by becoming powerful orators: "in the affairs of his city, showing how he may have most influence on public affairs both in speech and in action" (318e–319a). While the majority of society spends their lives fighting for survival with the weapons provided by Prometheus, Protagoras teaches the elite how they can use rhetoric to stand outside of the law like one of the Olympian deities. In spite of his supposed egalitarianism, Protagoras provides a philosophic justification for the rule of the strong over the weak. Although many people today would agree that the human being is the only arbiter of truth, realization of the unethical implications of this first principle invite us to reconsider the long tradition of philosophic thought that challenged this approach and denounced Protagoras.

Notes

Chapter 1

1 Although most sources identify Abdera as Protagoras' birthplace, Diogenes Laertius (9.8.50) cites one source that lists him as coming from Teos. This is most likely because Abdera was colonized by Teos in 544–545 BC (Herodotus 50.68; Peck 1898: 3).

2 See Plato, *Republic* 371e. For discussion, see Glotz (1967: 160–7).

3 Cf. Davison (1953: 38) who doubts that Protagoras actually worked as a porter.

4 Protagoras is credited with inventing a knot used to pack heavy loads (Diogenes Laertius 9.8.53; Smith et al. 1890: 407). It should be noted that some scholars questioned the validity of this anecdote since Protagoras was Democritus' elder by 20 years (Peck 1898: 1323; Davison 1953: 38).

5 Aelian (*Historical Miscellany* 1.23) refers to Protagoras as "son of Democritus."

6 For discussion, see Jaeger 1967: 20–1.

7 Also see Aristotle, *Metaphysics* 985b.

8 See Plato, *Theaetetus* 160c. For discussion of the human-measure fragment, see Schiappa 2003: 117–33.

9 Since Socrates was probably the most well-known philosopher in Athens, Aristophanes caricatures him in order to critique all intellectuals of the period.

10 For the association of the views expressed by Aristophanes' Socrates with Protagoras, see Corradi 2013: 74–5.

11 Diogenes Laertius (9.7.40) cites Aristoxenus for the claim that Plato had such disregard for Democritus that he had desired to burn all copies of his books. Additionally, he makes the observation that Plato never explicitly mentions Democritus in any of the dialogues despite discussing every other major philosopher of the period. Diogenes

believes this was an intentional oversight owing to Plato's inability to refute Democritus' philosophy.

12 Also see Diogenes Laertius 10.1.8.

13 Also see Plato, *Protagoras* 326c.

14 For discussion, see Muir 1982: 17–24; Fleming 2002: 18–25.

15 The brothers' association with Protagoras is likely as they were colonists of the city that Protagoras helped to found (Plato, *Euthydemus* 271c).

16 Protagoras was fond of comparisons between rhetoric and wrestling as suggested by the titles of several of his published works. Socrates indirectly refers to one of these, *Kataballontes Logoi* (Knockdown Arguments) at *Euthydemus* 277d, 288a. For discussion, see Hawee 2004: 51–3.

17 Also see Plato, *Meno* 92e; *Apology* 24e. Interestingly, Socrates sides with the sophists during his trial in defending his own sort of expertise as a gadfly stirring others to pursue virtue (Plato, *Apology* 25b, 30e); however, Socrates differentiates himself since he never accepted financial compensation for his instruction (*Apology* 19e).

18 My translation.

19 Aristotle defines *chremata* as "all those things whose value is measured by money" (*Nicomachean Ethics* 1119b).

20 This practice is also recounted by Aristotle (*Nicomachean Ethics* 1164a).

21 For discussion, see Lenzen 1977: 176–80.

22 The story is also recounted at Diogenes Laertius 9.8.56.

23 Since Socrates indicates that Protagoras had practiced sophistry for 40 years prior to his death, it is possible that his first visit to Athens was as early as 460 BC (Plato, *Meno* 91e). Davison (1953: 37) suggests that Protagoras' first visit to Athens was c. 444 BC, and Hippocrates indicates that considerable time has passed since this visit as he was too young to have met with him then (Plato, *Protagoras* 310e). Several scholars thus date the dramatic setting of Plato's *Protagoras* around 433 or 432 BC (Sauppe 1889: 7; Morrison 1941: 1–16; Davison 1953: 37). See also Athenaeus, *Deipnosophistae* 5.215c. Cf. Walsh (1984: 101–6) and Wolfsdorf (1997: 223–30) who both question the dominant position and argue that a definite date cannot be determined.

24 For discussion, see Roisman 2005.

25 For a complete portrait of Callias, see Freeman (1938: 20–35).

26 In addition to the accounts of Plato and Xenophon, Eupolis' lost play, *Flatterers* (421 BC), satirized Callias' indulgent lifestyle.

27 Stadter (1991: 114) doubts that Protagoras actually instructed Pericles' children. Compare Plato, *Protagoras* 319e–320a; *Meno* 94b.

28 The practice of having an esoteric teaching was common among many ancient philosophers including Plato and Aristotle. For evidence of Protagoras' having two sets of teaching, see Plato, *Theaetetus* 152c; *Protagoras* 316b. Many scholars read the "secret doctrine" referred to in *Theaetetus* simply within the context of Plato's argument rather than connecting it with the wider practice of esotericism.

29 For this understanding of the human-measure fragment, see Plato, *Theaetetus* 167c.

Chapter 2

1 The claim that Plato copied the entirety of the *Republic* from Protagoras' *Controversies* is provocative especially since the Platonic dialogue is largely motivated by an attempt to refute the sophistic position. It should also be noted that Socrates advanced a ruthless critique of democracy in book 9 of the dialogue. I speculate that this contradiction can be explained if the sophistic arguments advanced by Thrasymachus and Glaucon within the dialogue were taken from Protagoras' work, but not those advanced in Socrates' refutation of these ideas.

2 Farrar (1989: 45) suggests that Protagoras may have spent much of the 450s in Athens.

3 It should be noted that while Athenian democracy achieved a greater level of political and cultural participation for its male citizens than most modern democracies, no such rights were granted to women or slaves.

4 For discussion, see Robinson (2011: 140–5).

5 Democritus is one of the few other ancient philosophers besides Protagoras to have supported democracy. Although this sentiment is

reflected in some of the surviving fragments, there is no evidence that he provided a systematic defense of this form of government in the manner of Protagoras.

6 One should note that Protagoras violates this principle in the mythic section of the "Great Speech." For discussion, see Lampert (2010: 60–1).

7 See Farrar (1988: 76–7).

8 See also Plato, *Theaetetus* 167c.

9 O'Sullivan reports that this is the only other instance of this phrase found in a computer database search of extant Greek literature.

10 This date is derived from a statement in the *Meno*. Socrates tells us at 91e that Protagoras had been practicing sophistry for more than 40 years before his death in 420 BC.

11 It should be noted that my analysis of Pericles relies heavily on Plutarch's first-century AD biography of him. Although Plutarch is an invaluable source for information about ancient Greek and Roman historical figures, one should keep in mind that he was writing a good 500 years after Pericles lived.

12 See also Plutarch, *Aristides* 1.7; *Nicias* 6.1; Plato, *Laches* 197d. For discussion, see Lynch 2013.

13 Like many ancient historians, Plutarch may have composed the speech that he attributes to Protagoras. Even if the passage is more Plutarch's invention than a direct quote, one imagines he based this on some surviving testimony of the speech.

14 Plutarch (*Pericles* 36.4–5) presents a slightly different account of Pericles' stoicism indicating that he did lose his composure when laying a wreath on the grave of his remaining legitimate son, Paralus.

15 The Lyceum was significantly expanded as part of Pericles' many public works projects (*Suda* lambda, 802; Smith 1872: 258).

16 Kagan (1998: 170) also finds Protagoras' influence upon Pericles' religious views as expressed in the quoted passage from Plutarch. Cf. Stadter (1991: 114–15), who affirms Pericles' orthodoxy and dismisses any association with Protagoras' heretical views. However, the fact that the Athenians charged several of Pericles' closest associates with impiety suggests that there were legitimate concerns about his religious views.

17 See Plutarch, *Solon* 13. For a detailed discussion of the debate
    surrounding Athenian democracy, see Roberts 1997.
18 The funeral oration was delivered in 430 BC at the end of the first
    year of the Peloponnesian War. Although there is significant scholarly
    debate regarding the authenticity of the various speeches presented in
    Thucydides, Kagan (1991: xi–xii) argues for the authenticity of Pericles'
    speeches since Thucydides was in attendance during each of these.
    Roberts (1997: 41) argues that the funeral oration, in particular, should
    be trusted given how many people were in attendance when it was
    delivered. For a summary of the arguments suggesting that the speech
    was a later construction by Thucydides, see Asimopulos (2011: 233–9).
19 Saxonhouse (2006: 42–3) argues that Pericles offers only a perfunctory
    mention of the ancestors in his funeral oration and thus is rejecting
    tradition.
20 See also Plato, *Menexenus* 238c–d.
21 The date of the trial against Protagoras is disputed and may be as late as
    411 BC.
22 For the association between Oedipus and the philosophic
    enlightenment, see Goux 1993.

Chapter 3

1 Since the majority of the discussion that follows will be based on an
   interpretation of Plato's *Protagoras*, all subsequent citations to this work
   will simply note the relevant line numbers.
2 For discussion, see Strauss 1980.
3 For a valuable discussion of free speech in the context of ancient Greek
   society, see Saxonhouse 2006. Two chapters of Saxonhouse's work are
   devoted to the issue of free speech in Plato's *Protagoras*.
4 Also see Plato, *Republic* 600c. Cf. Adam (1905: 94), who dismisses the
   claim in *Theaetetus* that Protagoras actually had a secret teaching.
5 Diogenes Laerteus (9.8.55) includes in his listing of Protagoras'
   published works the title, *Of the Ancient Order of Things*—a likely
   source on which Plato based the "Great Speech." This title leads many

scholars to treat the "Great Speech" as a faithful account of Protagoras' ideas; for example, see Jaeger (1967: 189–90); Guthrie (1971: 63); Romilly (1992: 162); Schiappa (2003: 146–8); Beresford (2013: 143).

6 For this view, see Romilly (1992: 162); Rademaker (2013: 107). Romilly (1992: 176), recognizes that there were immoral sophists, but considers Protagoras to have had noble intentions and to have legitimately promoted morality.

7 Protagoras suggests at 323b that an individual's public declaration of his moral rectitude is not an accurate indicator of his true motives.

8 For the view that this is Protagoras' intention, see Segvic (2009: 14).

9 My translation.

10 Also see Plato, *Phaedrus* 267c. The ancient Greek language classifies nouns into three grammatical genders: masculine, feminine, and neuter. There is often no logical correlation between the grammatical gender of a word and its referent. Protagoras appears to be suggesting that words should be reclassified so that their linguistic gender agrees with their referent. He thus argues that *pelex* (helmet) should be grammatically masculine, presumably since it is something worn by men in the context of war. For discussion, see Kerferd (198: 68–77); Ophuijsen et al. (2013: 89–92).

11 Also see Drozdek 2005.

12 See also Hemmenway (1996: 2); Gonzalez (2000: 120–2).

13 See Guthrie (1971: 65), who notes the absence of the gods in the rational section of the "Great Speech."

14 Adkins (1973: 12) identifies Protagoras' speech as a "smoke screen" in which he completely violates his claim not to conceal his ideas.

15 For Socrates' further investigation of this issue, see Plato, *Meno*.

16 See Glaucon's similar conception of the self-interested origins of justice and social solidarity at Plato, *Republic* 358e–359a. Given the similarity of ideas, it is possible that Plato drew on Protagoras' thought when composing Glaucon's speech. This would also help explain the ancient claim that Protagoras had composed much of the *Republic*.

17 For this reading of the myth, see Beresford (2013: 139–62).

18 For the notion of justice as giving to each what is owed, see Plato, *Republic* 331e.

19 Compare Callicles' argument at Plato, *Gorgias* 482e–484c.
20 A translation of this work can be found in Sprague 1972.

Bibliography

Adam, J. *Platonis Protagoras*. Cambridge: Cambridge University Press, 1905.

Adkins, A. W. H. "*Arete, Techne*, Democracy, and Sophists: *Protagoras* 316b–328d," *Journal of Hellenic Studies* 93 (1973): 3–12.

Aelian. *Historical Miscellany*, trans. N. G. Wilson. Cambridge, MA: Harvard University Press, 1997.

Aelianus, C. *His Various History*, trans. T. Stanley. London: Thomas Dring, 1665. Accessed online.

Andocides. "Speeches," in *Minor Attic Orators*, vol. I, trans. K. J. Maidment. Cambridge, MA: Harvard University Press, 1941.

Antiphon. "Speeches," in *Minor Attic Orators*, vol. I, trans. K. J. Maidment. Cambridge, MA: Harvard University Press, 1941.

Apollodorus. *Apollodorus, The Library*, trans. J. G. Frazier. Cambridge, MA: Harvard University Press, 1921.

Aristophanes. "Clouds," in *Four Texts on Socrates: Plato's Euthyphro, Apology, and Aristophanes' Clouds*, trans. T. G. West and G. S. West. Ithaca, NY: Cornell University Press, 1998.

Aristotle. *Rhetoric*, trans. J. H. Freese. Cambridge, MA: Harvard University Press, 1926.

Aristotle. *De Sophisticis Elenchis (On Sophistical Refutations)*, trans. W. A. Pickard. Cambridge: Cambridge University Press, 1928.

Aristotle. *Metaphysics*, trans. H. Tredennick. Cambridge, MA: Harvard University Press, 1933.

Aristotle. *Nicomachean Ethics*, trans. H. Rackham. Cambridge, MA: Harvard University Press, 1934.

Aristotle. *Athenian Constitution; Eudemian Ethics; Virtues and Vices*, trans. H. Rackham. Cambridge, MA: Harvard University Press, 1935.

Aristotle. *Politics*, trans. H. Rackham. Cambridge, MA: Harvard University Press, 1944.

Asimopulos, P. "The Authenticity of Pericles' Funeral Oration in the European Historic Thought," *Facta Universitatis: Philosophy, Sociology, Psychology and History* 10 (2) (2011): 233–9.

Athenaeus. *Deipnosophistae*, vol. IV, trans. C. Burton. Cambridge, MA: Harvard University Press, 1930.

Beresford, A. "Fangs, Feathers, & Fairness: Protagoras on the Origins of Right and Wrong," in J. Ophuijsen, M. Raalte, and P. Stork, *Protagoras of Abdera, the Man, His Measure*, 139–62. Leiden: Brill Academic, 2013.

Cartledge, P. *Ancient Greek Political Thought in Practice*. New York: Cambridge University Press, 2009.

Corradi M. "*Ton Hēttō Logon Kreittō Poiein*: Aristotle, Plato, and the *Epangelma* of Protagoras," in J. Ophuijsen, M. Raalte, and P. Stork, *Protagoras of Abdera, the Man, His Measure*, 69–86. Leiden: Brill Academic, 2013.

Cuberley, E. P. *The History of Education: Educational Practice and Progress Considered as a Phase of the Development and the Spread of Western Civilization*. New York: Houghton Mifflin, 1920.

Davison, J. A. "Protagoras, Democritus, and Anaxagoras," *The Classical Quarterly* 3.1–2 (1953): 33–45.

Demosthenes. *Demosthenes*, trans. J. H. Vince. Cambridge, MA: Harvard University Press, 1930.

Diogenes Laertius. *Lives of Eminent Philosophers*, vol. I, trans. R. D. Hicks. Cambridge, MA: Harvard University Press, 1925.

Drozdek, A. "Protagoras and Instrumentality of Religion," *L'antiquité Classique* 74 (2005): 41–50.

Ehrenberg, V. "The Foundation of Thurii," *The American Journal of Philology* 69.2 (1948): 149–70.

Epictetus. *Discourses, Books 3–4; Fragments; The Encheiridion*, trans. W. A. Oldfather. Cambridge, MA: Harvard University Press, 1928.

Farrar, C. *The Origins of Democratic Thinking: The Invention of Politics in Classical Athens*. New York: Cambridge University Press, 1988.

Finley, M. I. *Democracy Ancient and Modern*. New Brunswick, NJ: Rutgers University Press, 1987.

Fleming, D. "The Streets of Thurii: Discourse, Democracy, and Design in the Classical Polis," *Rhetoric Society Quarterly* 32.3 (2002): 5–32.

Freeman, K. "Portrait of a Millionaire—Callias Son of Hipponicus," *Greece & Rome* 8.22 (1938): 20–35.

Freeman, K. (ed). *Ancilla to the Pre-Socratic Philosophers*. Cambridge, MA: Harvard University Press, 1983.

Gellius. *Attic Nights*, vol. 1, trans. J. C. Rolfe. Cambridge, MA: Harvard University Press, 1927.

Glotz, G. *Ancient Greece at Work: An Economic History of Greece from the Homeric Period to the Roman Conquest*, trans. M. R. Dobie. New York: W. W. Norton, 1967.

Gonzalez, F. "Giving Thought to the Good Together: Virtue in Plato's *Protagoras*," in *Retracing the Platonic Text*, J. Russon and J. Sallis, eds. Evanston, IL: Northwestern University Press, 2000.

Goux, J. J. *Oedipus, Philosopher*, trans. C. Porter. Stanford: Stanford University Press, 1993.

Guthrie, W. K. C. *The Sophists*. Cambridge: University of Cambridge Press, 1971.

Hanson, V. D. *The Other Greeks: The Family Farm and the Agrarian Roots of Western Civilization*. Berkeley: University of California Press, 1999.

Hawee, D. *Bodily Arts: Rhetoric and Athletics in Ancient Greece*. Austin: University of Texas Press, 2004.

Hemmenway, S. "Sophistry Exposed: Socrates on the Unity of Virtue in the *Protagoras*," *Ancient Philosophy* 16 (1996): 1–23.

Homer. *The Iliad of Homer*, trans. R. Lattimore. Chicago: University of Chicago Press, 1951.

Isocrates. *Antidosis*, trans. G. Morlin. Cambridge, MA: Harvard University Press, 1980.

Jaeger, W. *The Theology of the Early Greek Philosophers*. New York: Oxford University Press, 1967.

Kagan, D. *Pericles Of Athens And The Birth Of Democracy*. New York: The Free Press, 1991.

Kerferd, G. B. *The Sophistic Movement*. Cambridge: Cambridge University Press, 1981.

Lampert, L. *How Philosophy Became Socratic: A Study of Plato's Protagoras, Charmides, and Republic*. Chicago, IL: University of Chicago Press, 2012.

Landemore, H. *Democratic Reason: Politics, Collective Intelligence, and the Rule of the Many*. Princeton, NJ: Princeton University Press, 2013.

Lenzen, W. "Protagoras Versus Euathlus–Reflections on a So-called Paradox," *Ratio-New Series* 19.2 (1977): 176–80.

Liddell, H. G. and Scott, R. *A Greek-English Lexicon*, revised by H. S. Jones. Oxford: Clarendon Press, 1940.

Lynch, T. "A Sophist 'in Disguise': A Reconstruction of Damon of Oa and his Role in Plato's Dialogues," *Études platoniciennes* 10 (2013). Accessed online.

Lysias. *Lysias*, trans. W. R. M. Lamb. Cambridge, MA: Harvard University Press, 1930.

Morrison, J. S. "The Place of Protagoras in Athenian Public Life (460–415 B.C.)," *The Classical Quarterly* 35.1–2 (1941): 1–16.

Muir, J. V. "Protagoras and Education at Thourioi," *Greece & Rome* 29.1 (1982): 17–24.

O'Sullivan, N. "Pericles and Protagoras," *Greece & Rome* 42.1 (1995): 15–23.

Peck, H. T. *Harper's Dictionary of Classical Antiquity*. New York: Harper and Brothers, 1898.

Philostratus and Eunapius. *The Lives of the Sophists*, trans. W. C. Wright. Cambridge, MA: Harvard University Press, 1961.

Plato and Sauppe, H. *Protagoras, with the Commentary of Hermann Sauppe*, trans. J. A. Towle. Boston, MA: Ginn & Company, 1889.

Plato. *Theaetetus, Sophist*, trans. H. N. Fowler. Cambridge, MA: Harvard University Press, 1921.

Plato. *Laches, Protagoras, Meno, Euthydemus*, trans. W. R. M. Lamb. Cambridge, MA: Harvard University Press, 1924.

Plato. *Lysis, Symposium, Gorgias*, trans. W. R. M. Lamb. Cambridge, MA: Harvard University Press, 1925.

Plato. *Cratylus, Parmenides, Greater Hippias, Lesser Hippias*, trans. H. N. Fowler. Cambridge, MA: Harvard University Press, 1926.

Plato. *Charmides, Alcibiades I and II, Hipparchus, The Lovers, Theages, Minos, Epinomis*, trans. W. R. M. Lamb. Cambridge, MA: Harvard University Press, 1927.

Plato. *Timaeus, Critias, Cleitophon, Menexenus, Epistles*, trans. R. G. Bury. Cambridge, MA: Harvard University Press, 1929.

Plato. *Euthyphro, Apology, Crito, Phaedo*, trans. H. N. Fowler. Cambridge, MA: Harvard University Press, 1966.

Plato. *Republic*, trans. P. Shorey. Cambridge, MA: Harvard University Press, 1969.

Plutarch. *Plutarch's Lives*, trans. B. Perrin. Cambridge, MA: Harvard University Press, 1916.

Plutarch. "Consolatio ad Apollonium," in *Moralia*, vol. 2, trans. F. C. Babbitt. Cambridge, MA: Harvard University Press, 1928.

"Protagoras." *Suda on Line: Byzantine Lexicography*, trans. M. Heath. Lexington, KY: Stoa Consortium, 1999. Accessed online.

Rademaker, A. "The Most Correct Account: Protagoras on language," in J. Ophuijsen, M. Raalte, and P. Stork, *Protagoras of Abdera, the Man, His Measure*, 87–112. Leiden: Brill Academic, 2013.

Roberts, J. T. *Athens on Trial: The Antidemocratic Tradition in Western Thought*. Princeton, NJ: Princeton University Press, 1997.

Robinson, E. W. "The Sophists and Democracy beyond Athens," *Rhetorica: A Journal of the History of Rhetoric* 25.1 (2007): 109–22.

Robinson, E. W. *Democracy Beyond Athens: Popular Government in the Greek Classical Age*. Cambridge: Cambridge University Press, 2011.

Roisman, J. *The Rhetoric of Manhood: Masculinity in the Attic Orators*. Berkeley, CA: University of California Press, 2005.

Romilly, J. de. *The Great Sophists in Periclean Athens*, trans. J. Lloyd. Oxford: Oxford University Press, 1992.

Saxonhouse, A. *Free Speech and Democracy in Ancient Athens*. Cambridge: Cambridge University Press, 2006.

Schiappa, E. *Protagoras and Logos: A Study in Greek Philosophy and Rhetoric*. Columbia, SC: University of South Carolina Press, 2003.

Sedvic, H. *From Protagoras to Aristotle: Essays in Ancient Moral Philosophy*. Princeton, NJ: Princeton University Press, 2009.

Seneca. *Ad Lucilium Epistulae Morales*, vol. II, trans. R. M. Gummere. Cambridge, MA: Harvard University Press, 1953.

Smith, W. *A Dictionary of Greek and Roman Biography*. Boston: Little, Brown, 1844.

Smith, W., Wayte, W., and Marindin, G. E. *A Dictionary of Greek and Roman Antiquities*. London: J. Murray, 1890.

Sophocles. *The Oedipus Tyrannus of Sophocles*, trans. R. Jebb. Cambridge: Cambridge University Press, 1887.

Sprague, R. *The Older Sophists: A Complete Translation by Several Hands of the Fragments in Die Fragmente der Vorsokratiker*. Columbia: University of South Carolina Press, 1972.

Stadter, P. A. "Pericles Among the Intellectuals," *Illinois Classical Studies* 16.1–2 (1991): 111–24.

Strauss, L. *Persecution and the Art of Writing*. Chicago, IL: University of Chicago Press, 1980.

Theognis. "Elegies," in *Hesiod and Theognis*, trans. D. Wender. London: Penguin Books, 1973.

Thucydides. *The Landmark Thucydides: A Comprehensive Guide to the Peloponnesian War*, R. B. Strassler and V. D. Hanson, eds., trans. R. Crawley. New York: The Free Press, 1998.

Versenyi, L. "Protagoras' Man-measure Fragment," *The American Journal of Philology* 83.2 (1962): 178–84.

Walsh, J. "The Dramatic Dates of Plato's Protagoras and the Lesson of Arete," *The Classical Quarterly* 34.1 (1984): 101–6.

Waterfield, R. *The First Philosophers: The Presocratics and Sophists*. Oxford: Oxford University Press, 2000.

Wolfsdorf, D. "The Dramatic Date of Plato's Protagoras," *Rheinisches Museum für Philologie* 140.3–4 (1997): 223–30.

Xenophon. *Memorabilia, Oeconomicus, Symposium*, trans. E. C. Marchant. Cambridge, MA: Harvard University Press, 1923.

Index